WHAT PEOPI
IT'S N

Proverbs tells us that the glory of kings is found in their searching. For years, Cameron has searched the world, gleaning wisdom from diverse cultures, experiences, and thought leaders. If you're looking to elevate your leadership, following Cameron in his exploration is the perfect path. Cameron's unique blend of real-world experience and profound understanding offers a blueprint for leadership that is both visionary and deeply rooted in integrity. Dive in and discover how to lead with the wisdom of a king.

—Jeremy Cleveland
Lead Pastor, Zeal City Church

There are two words that describe this book: transparent and authentic. I firmly believe that these two characteristics built upon integrity create great leaders. I have known Cameron for a little over a year but have learned a lot about him in this book. Far too many authors are quick to point out the mistakes that others make and not their own. This is not the case with Cameron—he is quick to point out the mistakes he has made and the lessons he has learned. When the leader is transparent and authentic, others willingly follow, and they are open to learning from the leader. This is a good book for those who aspire to be a leader and for those who are leading.

—Rick Davis
Retired Battalion Chief, Loveland Fire Rescue Authority
Author of *The Furnace of Leadership Development*

Cameron is one of the most dedicated men I know when it comes to leadership and personal growth. He has a hunger to be the best version of himself and an intense desire to learn. He leads by action instead of words. The stories and concepts presented in this book have come over a lifetime of growth and are delivered in a way that is immediately applicable to your life. This book will be worth your time!

—Jonathan McGinley
Owner of Intentional Man, Host of *The Intentional Man Podcast*

I first met Cameron in college at San Jose State and had the privilege of witnessing many of his early accomplishments. I am grateful for his ability to influence those around him through his shared experience. His authenticity has always resonated, and I took refuge in knowing I was not alone. I am thrilled to see him expand his circle of influence to a new and broader audience.

—Alfredo Lopez-Ruiz
Leader in the Business Aviation Industry

Cameron Singh's book, *It's Not About You*, is a powerful guide for aspiring young leaders who want to be salt and light leaders in the marketplace. Singh's personal experiences and insights provide valuable lessons on the importance of integrity, humility, and a deepening relationship with God. His emphasis on being in it with your team and leading responsibly is a refreshing perspective in a world where self-promotion often takes precedence. I highly recommend this book to anyone looking to enhance their leadership skills and create a positive impact in their sphere of influence.

—Don Overcash
Former City Councilor and Mayor Pro-Tem for Loveland, CO
President of Overcash Consulting

I've had the pleasure of knowing Cameron Singh professionally and personally, and his journey as a leader has always impressed me. Cameron's new book captures his authentic and thoughtful approach to leadership, providing readers with a wealth of insights drawn from his own experiences. Cameron's reflections and advice are a valuable guide for anyone looking to lead with integrity and purpose.

—Ben Garey
CEO of Capstone Aero

I have had the privilege of knowing Cameron for quite some time. Cameron's leadership is unparalleled. I have continuously seen him adeptly navigate challenges and inspire his team to excellence. His vision, integrity, and dedication make him an exceptional leader. Cameron's impact extends far beyond the workplace, leaving an indelible mark on all who have the privilege of knowing him.

—Daniel Gelman
Airline Pilot

Having had the privilege of mentoring Cameron, I am thrilled to see his wisdom and insights captured in this notable book on leadership. Cameron masterfully explores the critical pillars of successful leadership: people, process, and product. His profound understanding of how to nurture talent, optimize operations, and deliver outstanding results is both inspiring and practical. This book is a must-read for anyone aspiring to lead with excellence and drive impactful change. Cameron's journey and expertise are a testament to his dedication and innovative thinking. I highly recommend this book to leaders at all levels.

—Pasquale Raguseo
Senior Leader in the Business Aviation Industry

Cameron gets it! Many leaders, as I've discovered throughout thirty years of coaching, are "overexposed" and "underdeveloped!" In other words, the development they need to lead well often doesn't match the assignments God has given them. This is Cameron's driving passion. In a winsome, humble, and transparent way, he shares from his personal journey the principles and tools that you will need to find your why and your way forward to be better equipped for your current and future leadership callings.

—Dan Anderson
President/CEO of Kingdom Way Ministries
National Ministry Director of FCCI

I'm excited to endorse this fantastic book by my good friend Cameron Singh. Growing alongside Cameron as a growth accountability partner, I've seen his outstanding leadership skills firsthand. This book is packed with wisdom for young professionals to avoid common mistakes that keep them from succeeding. It's a must-read for anyone looking to develop and lead effectively.

—Travis Vandeusen
Small Business and Organizational Leadership
Advisor, Upstream Benefits Group

Leadership has always been a topic of immense fascination and critical importance. As I reflect on the journey of leadership, both in my own experiences and in the numerous stories I have encountered, it becomes clear that true leadership is an ever-evolving art, rooted in integrity, vision, and the relentless pursuit of excellence.

In the pages that follow, Cameron Singh offers a profound exploration of what it means to be an effective leader in today's complex world. This book is not just a collection of theories and principles but a comprehensive guide that intertwines practical wisdom with inspiring anecdotes, providing a roadmap for aspiring, new, and seasoned leaders alike.

One of the key strengths of this book is Cameron's ability to distill the essence of leadership into relatable and actionable insights. Whether you are leading a small team, an entire organization, or simply striving to lead your own life with greater purpose and clarity, the lessons contained within these chapters will resonate deeply and provide valuable guidance.

Throughout this book, you will find a rich tapestry of leadership concepts, from the importance of emotional intelligence and the power of effective communication to the necessity of resilience and the art of strategic thinking. Each chapter is meticulously crafted to challenge your perspectives, ignite your passion, and empower you to lead with authenticity and confidence.

What sets this book apart is its emphasis on the human side of leadership, especially with the younger generations. Cameron understands that at the heart of every successful leader is the ability to connect with and inspire others. This book reminds us that leadership is not about wielding power, but about serving others, building trust, and fostering a culture of collaboration and innovation.

As you embark on this journey through the insights and stories presented in this book, I encourage you to reflect on your own leadership path. Embrace the challenges, celebrate the victories, and always strive to grow and evolve. Leadership is not a destination but a continuous journey of learning, growth, and impact.

I am confident that Cameron Singh's work will not only inspire you but will also equip you with the tools and mindset necessary to navigate the complexities of leadership in the modern world. May this book serve as a beacon of wisdom and a catalyst for your own leadership journey.

—Kenyatta Thomas
Business Aviation Industry Leader

No one in my life who pursues growth in leadership like Cameron Singh. He relentlessly pursues who God has made him to be as a leader, and this is reflected in this book. The examples, quotes, and connections that he makes will move all of us to a greater level of leadership if we are willing to let it.

—Josh Keller
Co-Owner of The Freedom Center MN

I've known Cameron Singh up close and personal in a variety of settings—large and small. I'm so glad he wrote *It's Not About You*, because in it, he writes about what I have observed and respected about him: his constant pursuit of growth, while not losing sight of himself as a leader. His resiliency and constant screening of core motivations have helped his success and will surely help you and your colleagues.

—Sam Chand
Leadership Consultant and author of *VOICES*

IT'S NOT ABOUT ~~YOU~~

Copyright © 2025 by Cameron Singh

Published by Dream Releaser Publishing

All rights reserved. No portion of this book may be reproduced, stored in a retrieval system, or transmitted in any form or by any means—electronic, mechanical, photocopy, recording, scanning, or other—except for brief quotations in critical reviews or articles, without prior written permission of the author.

Unless otherwise specified, all Scripture quotations are taken from the Holy Bible, New International Version®, NIV®. Copyright © 1973, 1978, 1984, 2011 by Biblica, Inc.™ Used by permission of Zondervan. All rights reserved worldwide. www.zondervan.com. The "NIV" and "New International Version" are trademarks registered in the United States Patent and Trademark Office by Biblica, Inc.™ | Scripture quotations marked ESV are from The ESV® Bible (The Holy Bible, English Standard Version®), copyright © 2001 by Crossway, a publishing ministry of Good News Publishers. Used by permission. All rights reserved. | Scripture quotations marked NKJV are taken from the New King James Version®. Copyright © 1982 by Thomas Nelson. Used by permission. All rights reserved. | Scripture quotations marked NLT are taken from the Holy Bible, New Living Translation, copyright © 1996, 2004, 2015 by Tyndale House Foundation. Used by permission of Tyndale House Publishers, Inc., Carol Stream, Illinois 60188. All rights reserved.

For foreign and subsidiary rights, contact the author.

Cover design by Sara Young
Cover photo by Andrew van Tilborgh

ISBN: 978-1-960678-11-9   1 2 3 4 5 6 7 8 9 10

Printed in the United States of America

CAMERON NATHAN SINGH

IT'S NOT ABOUT YOU

WHY NEW LEADERS CAN'T (AND SHOULDN'T) LEAD ALONE

To my amazing family, Cheyanne (sister), Mom (Esther), Dad (Jack), and grandparents (Suruj and Siri) who have always supported me in my journey each step of the way. It is because of your faith and belief in me that I have been able to pursue such incredible opportunities and experience life to the fullest. I would not be where I am today if it were not for your belief and encouragement in my life!

I dedicate this book to each of you and my God who has never failed me. He has always been there even when I thought He wasn't.

CONTENTS

Foreword xv

Acknowledgments xix

Introduction 21

CHAPTER 1. **YOU HAVE INFLUENCE. YOU ARE A LEADER!** 25

CHAPTER 2. **YOUR WHY** 37

CHAPTER 3. **PEOPLE, PRODUCT, PROCESS.** 53

CHAPTER 4. **DEFINING YOUR LEADERSHIP STYLE AND PATH** 63

CHAPTER 5. **TAKE RISKS** 75

CHAPTER 6. **BE BOLD IN FAITH** 87

CHAPTER 7. **GET OUT OF YOUR COMFORT ZONE AND SET YOURSELF APART** 91

CHAPTER 8. **PURSUE GROWTH IN FAITH** 101

CHAPTER 9. **LEAD RESPONSIBLY IN FAITH** 111

CHAPTER 10. **REMAIN HUMBLE IN FAITH** 121

CHAPTER 11. **LEARN FROM LEADERS** 131

CHAPTER 12. **DON'T LOSE YOURSELF IN LEADERSHIP** 139

CHAPTER 13. **CONTINUAL DEVELOPMENT AND EDUCATION** 145

FINAL THOUGHTS **DON'T GIVE UP. PRESS ON. KEEP LEADING.** 149

Appendix 153

About the Author 155

FOREWORD

It is with great pleasure and heartfelt honor that I write this foreword for Cameron's second book, a reflection of his remarkable journey from an up-and-coming leader to the thoughtful, dedicated, and transparent leader he is today. My name is Steve, and I have had the unique privilege of witnessing Cameron's growth and transformation from his very first leadership role to his current status as a respected and admired leader. Our relationship has evolved from professional acquaintance to a deep and enduring friendship, one that I cherish dearly.

I first met Cameron when he was stepping into his initial leadership role. Like many young leaders, he was filled with enthusiasm but also faced the daunting challenge of navigating uncharted waters. It was clear from the beginning that Cameron possessed a natural inclination towards leadership. He had an innate ability to connect with people and inspire those around him. However, like all of us, his early days were marked by a mixture of successes and learning experiences.

What has always stood out about Cameron is his relentless commitment to personal growth. He embraced every challenge as an opportunity to learn and improve, demonstrating a level of humility and self-awareness that is rare in leaders of any age. He understood that leadership is not about having all the answers but about fostering an environment where everyone can contribute their best ideas and efforts.

As Cameron progressed in his career, I had the pleasure of seeing him take on more significant responsibilities. With each new role, his leadership style evolved. He became more thoughtful in his decision-making, more dedicated to his team's development, and more transparent in his communication. Cameron's dedication to leading with integrity and authenticity has been inspiring to witness. He has always been willing to share his own experiences, both triumphs and setbacks, to help others navigate their paths.

One of the defining moments in Cameron's leadership journey was when he embraced the principle of servant leadership. He realized that true leadership is about serving others and putting the needs of the team and the organization above his own. This shift in mindset allowed him to build stronger, more cohesive teams and to create a culture of trust and mutual respect. Cameron's ability to listen, empathize, and support his team members has made a profound impact on all who have had the privilege of working with him.

Cameron's transparency as a leader has also been a cornerstone of his success. He has never shied away from difficult conversations or from acknowledging his own mistakes. By being open and honest, he has fostered a culture where team members feel safe to express their ideas and concerns. This transparency has not only built trust within his teams but has also driven innovation and continuous improvement in all the environments that he has led.

Over the years, Cameron and I have shared countless discussions about leadership, personal development, and life. These conversations have deepened my respect for him not only as a leader but as a person. Cameron is someone who genuinely cares about others and is committed to making a positive difference in the world. His dedication to his faith, his family, and his community is unwavering, and he leads by example in every aspect of his life.

In this book, Cameron shares his leadership journey with an honesty and vulnerability that is both refreshing and inspiring. He provides valuable insights and practical advice for aspiring leaders, new leaders, and even seasoned leaders who are looking to grow. Cameron's story is a testament to the power of perseverance, continuous learning, and staying true to one's values, including his faith.

As you read this book, I encourage you to take to heart the lessons that Cameron has learned along the way. His journey is a powerful reminder that leadership is not a destination but a continuous journey of growth and self-discovery. Whether you are just starting out in your leadership career or looking to refine your skills, Cameron's experiences and reflections will provide you with the guidance and inspiration you need.

Cameron, thank you for sharing your story with us. Your journey is a beacon of hope and encouragement for leaders everywhere. I am proud to call you my friend and I am excited to see where your leadership journey will take you next.

With deepest respect and admiration,
—Steve Akin, Business Owner

ACKNOWLEDGMENTS

Wow, I can't believe this is my second book. During the journey of writing this book, there were many trials and tribulations I faced in every aspect of my life. The most difficult part of writing this was believing in myself, but there were so many who encouraged me to continue writing, and many have been waiting for this book.

I am so thankful for God who stayed by my side throughout this journey and through the experiences I share in this book. I am so appreciative of my amazing family who supported me during the good days and the hard days. I'm grateful they have supported all my ambitions and pursuits even though they sometimes thought I was crazy. Despite that, their support has been unwavering and has inspired me to reach for higher and higher.

So many individuals and mentors have given me their time throughout my leadership journey. If it wasn't for their time and mentorship, I would not have been in leadership roles at such a young age. I value all who have sacrificed their time amid their busy schedules!

A special thank you to my publisher, Dream Releaser Publishing and Four Rivers Media. I am very thankful for the partnership in helping me package a dear message that God laid on my heart to help inspire and impact others seeking a life in leadership. Thank you for your patience as I faced trials and tribulations I would have never imagined. You are rock stars, and I greatly appreciate your diligent support on this project.

Sam Chand, thank you for your continued encouragement both from a distance and in person at your year-round leadership events. You sent me a text a while ago that said "I believe in YOU," and that meant the world to me. I continue to be encouraged by you, your books, and the people who surround you.

INTRODUCTION

I have been so passionate about leadership from a very young age. At the time, people well older than I was at the time held these various leadership roles that so deeply fascinated me. I knew nothing about leadership when I landed my first role. In episode 109 of a podcast I co-host called *The Leadership Download Podcast*, I had the opportunity to interview performance coach and keynote speaker Jordan Montgomery. He talked about being overexposed and underdeveloped when he was promoted to leadership roles in his twenties. In that interview, he mentioned that leadership can be messy with several bumps along the way... which is so true![1]

My first book, *Navigation and Discovery*, told the story of my high school and college years when I was trying to figure everything out. It also shed light on my faith journey and how that evolved with many challenges along the way.[2] Here, I want to share my first leadership experiences and what I learned. Stepping into a leadership role for the first time can be very intimidating, and the environment you are in may not set you up for success or equip you with the resources you need to be a successful leader.

---
1 Jordan Montgomery, "The Journey of Success in Your Youth," *Leadership Download Podcast*, April 10, episode 109, https://open.spotify.com/episode/31V3GMgsmzC5FyS4HcxguY?si=0896d82778b94820.
2 Singh, *Navigation and Discovery*.

I hope this will be a useful resource for you, whether you are an aspiring leader, a new leader, or even a seasoned leader. Wherever we are in our leadership journeys, we can always use a little help and guidance.

My "why" has been very important to me as I've stepped into leadership roles. I have seen many leaders change for the worse after a promotion. The leadership role got to their head and their motives shifted. A great Bible verse that speaks to this is Philippians 2:3-4 (ESV): "Do nothing from selfish ambition or conceit, but in humility count others more significant than yourselves. Let each of you look not only to his own interests but also to the interests of others." I will talk about balancing your interests and the interests of others in leadership at the beginning of the book.

I will share my experience in leadership and how I defined my leadership style and found my way through trial and error. The burdens of leadership can be very heavy, especially in your first leadership role. I went through challenges early on and had to learn to be bold, take risks, get out of my comfort zone, and set myself apart to further grow and develop in my leadership. I will share what it means to be a responsible leader because I have seen so many leaders fall short, become irresponsible, and ultimately ruin their careers. New and aspiring leaders need humility, and I will share my experiences with practicing humility—another major challenge in leadership roles. James 4:10 (NLT) says, "Humble yourselves before the Lord, and he will lift you up in honor."

I also find myself passionate about growth. Entering into your first leadership role does not mean you have made it. It is just the beginning of your leadership journey. Growing never stops. In leadership, you have to get better and better every day. This lesson has helped me tremendously in my leadership journey.

Lastly, I'll cover the importance of not losing yourself in leadership or giving up, but to press on. Leadership is not easy. As I mentioned earlier, leadership is messy, and it can make or break you. Don't let it break you because it broke me in more ways than you can imagine. I will share my journey of leadership where I lost sight of who I was because I was so immersed in "the doing" that my title became my identity.

I hope this book will encourage you that you have what it takes to lead. You can do it. You can grow as a leader. You are a leader where you are now. I hope my story assures you that you are not alone and are more than capable of leading. It won't be an easy journey but with great intentionality, you can do it!

CHAPTER I

YOU HAVE INFLUENCE. YOU ARE A LEADER!

Influence.

What is it and how does it relate to leadership? Let's start by defining what influence is. According to Center for Creative Leadership, influence is "the ability to affect the behavior of others in a particular direction, leveraging key tactics that involve, connect, and inspire them."[3] I recall a session called "Spheres" at the Hillsong Conference in Sydney, Australia I attended over ten years ago. In this session, Pastor Joel A'Bell of Hillsong Church at the time, talked about how you have the power to make a difference and be a person of influence no matter who you are or where you are, whether it is in government, as a student, in the church, in business, etc. You have the power to make a difference and be a person of influence in every sphere of life. This message took me aback. I realized that I had the ability to influence others where I was in my career path at that time. This was the first time I had

---

[3] "How to Influence People: 4 Skills for Influencing Others," *Center for Creative Leadership*, 26 October 2023, https://www.ccl.org/articles/leading-effectively-articles/4-keys-strengthen-ability-influence-others/.

heard that you could be a person of influence and make an impact where you are right now. My title didn't mean anything. I have influence and have always had influence. Prior to this experience, I was under the assumption that I was never going to become something because of my circumstances, whether because of where I grew up in the small town of San Bruno, California, because I was a first-generation college student, or because I was of Indian descent. I think I limited myself based on my circumstances at the time, and I saw many others within my community and age group limiting themselves as well.

Hey, you. Yes, you—you have the power and ability to influence those around you. I remember I returned home to California after the Hillsong Conference with a changed mindset that I can influence and impact people where I am at. At this time, I was a few years into the workforce and in my first leadership role. I doubted myself a lot. I did not think I was worthy of leading people. I questioned myself on why people would want to listen to what I had to say. I'm only in my early twenties. How could people trust me to lead?

I then realized I don't need to be a pastor or in ministry to be a person of influence. I can influence where I am in business. You are the light of the world no matter your circumstances. I remember Pastor Erwin McManus at the Hillsong Conference speaking on "Spheres" and he mentioned you are not like any other species on this planet. He stated that you can see a future that does not exist, and you can dream of a world that we have never actually known. Furthermore, he said, God breathes his imagination into us, and we are God's creative agencies to create a future that God has in mind.

Upon hearing this, I reflected on the opportunities I had in the past for influence, and I realized it was a lot. In grade school, I was diligent when it came to homework and being the "teacher's pet," and so many of my classmates wanted to copy my work. Even in college, I was a mediocre student, but people were still interested in seeing how I did certain assignments and projects. They would ask me for help. Now I reflect, and wonder why so many people sought help from me whether it was copying my homework in grade school or seeking my guidance and help in college. I realized this stemmed from my focus on building relationships and loving people. I always put my attention on people no matter what their beliefs or walk of life. I expressed love towards them for who they were and continued to encourage them wherever they were without any judgment. I met them where they were just like God meets us where we are. I always have been known as the "nice guy" because I love on people so well.

Even the most timid and quiet people can have influence. The first impression you will get from me is that I am very timid, but once I get to know a person, I get more comfortable and open up. I am very selective yet intentional with my interactions. The timidness and quietness have helped me to understand and listen to other people better. These days, I have observed that people are slow to listen and quick to speak. I have found that people are more curious about what the reserved, timid, and quiet person has to say, and this gave me permission to speak and have influence in many situations during my early days in the workforce. Don't limit yourself. It's the worst thing you could do. I limited myself without even realizing it and once I overcame that, the opportunities were endless. The endless opportunities can be for you, too.

THE FOUNDATION OF INFLUENCE IS TRUST.

Influence is something I picked up from my parents and grandparents because they are all generous people who love other people so well. People would always come to our house on the weekends for dinner or tea, and many were not even family. My parents love on everyone whom they encounter. I was blessed to grow up close to my Nani and Nana (maternal grandparents), and I also observed them loving on people, from people at church to people at the grocery store! Many people, even those who were not family, would visit them. Generosity has been instilled in their DNA for as long as I have known them. I definitely took on my parents' and grandparents' traits as early as grade school. I remember sharing my lunch with my classmates who didn't bring food or sometimes giving away my lunch and go hungry. I did not realize that this was a form of influence. Looking back, I have always been others-focused without even realizing it because of my upbringing, which I am so grateful for. The foundation of influence is trust. And I continue to build great trust with the people around me.

I also learned influence from my Christian faith as God calls us to love on His people. He calls us to love our enemies and neighbors. In John 15:12-13, God says, "My command is this: Love each other as I have loved you. Greater love has no one than this: to lay down one's life for one's friends." God calls us to love just like He has loved us. Jesus is the ultimate example of influence. He was a carpenter and wasn't traditionally thought of as someone who was becoming something, but as the years went by, Jesus started to hone in and cherish His influence simply by loving on people one person at a time regardless of who they were and their walk of life.

Remember that your influence is always evolving. It is never static.[4] No matter who you are, where you are, what your position is, or what direction you are headed in life, you are both influencing and being influenced by others constantly. With influence comes great authority and responsibility, and how you handle that influence and how intentional you are with it are what makes the difference.

Think about all the influence you have right now where you are. You have influence with your family, your friends, your coworkers, your classmates, within your church, and everywhere you go on a day-to-day basis. You have so much influence—and you may not even know it. Sometimes I have found that just saying hello to someone at church or the grocery store while running errands makes an incredible impact on their lives and can make someone's day.

Take some time to pause and reflect on the kind of influence you have on others. Do you add value to every touchpoint with other people, whether it be in-person, by phone, text message, or social media? Just a simple DM or comment congratulating someone for a huge accomplishment is a form of influence. In today's world, people value time, and giving someone time through any means of communication is a form of influence.

Right now, you may doubt whether you have any influence or question whether you will become someone worthy of influencing

---

[4] Sam Chand, "Everyone Has Influence: Adding Value to Those Around You," *Medium*, 7 November 2019, https://medium.com/practical-leadership/everyone-has-influence-ddafb3381b6b.

others. I had those same thoughts. You have influence whether you mean to or not. It really takes intentionality to decide what kind of influence you want to have and with whom. And age does not matter. Whether you are thirteen or twenty-three or thirty-three, you have influence, and John C. Maxwell says that leadership is influence.[5]

Leadership is not a title. It's not position, it's not rank. It is influence.

Once I got this sense of awakening at Hillsong Conference back in 2016, it was like God lit a fire within me. It was then that I started to hear the terms "leadership" and "leader" and I started to get clarity on the meaning of leadership. Many of the pastors who spoke at the conference discussed leadership. If you read my book *Navigation and Discovery*, you will learn more about the impact the Hillsong Conference had on my life.[6] At the conference, Pastor Casey Treat spoke about our calling to be like Jesus, and that none of us have arrived yet. To get there, we need to live in the new and be open to change and renew our minds in order to move towards the direction He has called us to walk. He also encouraged us that we are all leaders no matter who or where we are.

LEADERSHIP IS NOT A TITLE. IT'S NOT POSITION, IT'S NOT RANK. IT IS INFLUENCE.

---

[5] John C. Maxwell, *The 21 Irrefutable Laws of Leadership: Follow Them and People Will Follow You* (Nashville, TN: HarperCollins, September 16, 2007).
[6] Singh, *Navigation and Discovery*.

Pastor Erwin McManus, another amazing speaker at the Hillsong Conference, mentioned that we are to go into every sphere and be the best educators, the best businesspeople, the best scientists, the best political leaders, and the best artists we can be to fulfill our calling as the lights of the world. At this point, I began to believe I had to strive to be the best of the best in whatever I pursued. But self-doubt was sinking in because I was only about twenty-five at the time. I questioned how I could be the best of the best at the age of twenty-five. I was then reminded of 1 Timothy 4:12 (ESV) which says, "Let no one despise you for your youth, but set the believers an example in speech, in conduct, in love, in faith, in purity."

I always wondered, *what is this influence and leadership thing that pastors are always talking about?* I started to watch their content on YouTube, listen to their podcasts, and lean into their messages about influence and leadership.

The following year in 2017, I attended a leadership conference called Catalyst. Several leadership champions spoke such as Brian Houston, Andy Stanley, Tim Tebow, Robert Madu, Christy Wright, Craig Groeschel, and Bob Goff. I had begun to follow these leaders throughout my journey. Much of what I heard stood out to me. Tim Tebow said, "People don't follow titles. They follow courage."[7] Brian Houston asked, "How do you lead with longevity in mind and build a team that lasts?"[8] He said that this is done through instilling a vision in your team to create space for individuals to flourish and fulfill their own visions.

---

7 Tim Tebow, "People don't follow titles. They follow courage," *2017 Catalyst Leadership Conference,* 16-17 June 2017, https://www.catalystleader.com.
8 Brian Houston, "How do you lead with longevity in mind and build a team that lasts?", *2017 Catalyst Leadership Conference,* 16-17 June 2017, https://www.catalystleader.com.

I wanted to learn more about leadership and influence as I listened to more of these leadership-focused talks and purchased more of their resources and books. I began to study the works of these speakers that I found through researching, listening to podcasts, and watching YouTube videos.

What I really want you to take away so far is that you have influence and because you have influence, you have the ability to lead no matter where you are. Yes, you have influence! I didn't find that out until flying all the way out to Sydney, Australia from San Francisco to attend Hillsong Conference.

You may not feel like a leader, and that's okay. You really won't feel like a leader until you have developed a great sense of self-awareness, which is truly the foundation of leading effectively.

UNDERSTANDING WHO WE ARE FIRST WILL INFORM WHAT WE DO OR HOW WE LEAD.

Influencing and impacting others comes from a place of authenticity, and it starts with self-awareness. In his book, *How to Lead When You're Not in Charge*, Clay Scroggins mentions that we have to understand our unique identity which requires a keen self-understanding of who we are as individuals and putting our titles aside.[9] Understanding who we are first will inform what we do or how we lead.

---

9 Clay Scroggins, *How to Lead When You're Not in Charge: Leveraging Influence When You Lack Authority* (Grand Rapids, MI: Zondervan, August 22, 2017).

In a *Catalyst* article, Tyler Reagin said to "remain a student to leadership by never giving up on learning about yourself."[10]

Before you decide how you influence others and the people around you, ask yourself, "Do I have a true understanding of who I am and my identity?"

This is something I struggled with early on when I started in the workforce and was promoted to leadership roles at a very young age. I started defining myself based on my title and what I did rather than staying true to myself and understanding my identity. It was a real struggle as I had an amazing leadership journey in my twenties working in the aviation industry, but I realized I had lost who I was. My identity was based on all the wins and affirmations at work, and believe me, there were wins after wins, promotion after promotion. It wasn't until living abroad that I began to discover my identity and true self.

I had the opportunity to live in the Caribbean for a few years on the beautiful twin island of Antigua and Barbuda. Upon starting my journey living in Antigua and Barbuda, I realized that the team I was leading and many others that I encountered had purpose beyond work such as faith, family, friendships, and culture. It opened my eyes that there's more to life than work and winning at work. After about a few months of learning about the culture in Antigua, I finally took a "chill pill" and started the journey of discovering my identity by creating balance and embracing my experience in the Caribbean. I became very social, more than ever, and made many great friends. I found new hobbies and honed in on my golf game. I read, journaled, prayed, and read

---

10 Tyler Reagin, "Leadership Lessons from the Green," *Catalyst*, https://insider.catalystleader.com/read/leadership-lessons-from-the-green.

the Bible to build my faith. I had a lot of time for reflection, and I completely changed my rhythm in my day-to-day life.

It doesn't mean I stopped winning at work. I still put in my all at work but focused on how I could better help my team each day rather than focus on my own wins. That was very rewarding, and I saw the fruits of shifting the focus off of me.

ASK FOR FEEDBACK AND CHERISH THAT FEEDBACK, EVEN IF YOU DON'T LIKE IT.

I found that journey of self-awareness starts with asking for feedback from those around you and then evaluating whether it aligns with what you think about yourself. There are many things I was not aware of that my friends, coworkers, and mentors shared. Ask for feedback and cherish that feedback, even if you don't like it. You will better understand and connect with others when you understand yourself and develop self-awareness. The Center for Creative Leadership mentions that the better you understand yourself, the better you'll understand others.[11] The University of Florida has contributed to this conversation of influence, as well. They agree that influence starts with building connections with others and understanding their needs, motivations, and values.[12]

---

[11] "4 Sure-Fire Ways to Boost Your Self-Awareness," *Center for Creative Leadership*, 20 February 2022, https://www.ccl.org/articles/leading-effectively-articles/4-ways-boost-self-awareness/.
[12] "Maximize Your Leadership Potential: Build Trust," *University of Florida Human Resources*, https://training.hr.ufl.edu/resources/LeadershipToolkit/job_aids/LeadingbyInfluence.pdf.

You will build greater influence by showing a sincere commitment to what matters to someone else as they realize your actions reflect a genuine concern for their interests.

With influence comes great power. It comes from an inner strength that invites people to listen to you and attracts them to work with you. The power of your influence encourages others to share your vision. I will cover this in future chapters but looking to your mentors and role models is a great place to start. An article in *BetterUp* says, "Once you grasp what it feels like to be inspired by people who've made a defining mark in your life, you have a sense for meaningful influence, person to person."[13] Before we dive into that, it is essential to know your why. You may not know your why, but I can help. What I want you to take from this chapter is this:

You have influence.
You have influence.
You have influence.

You have the power of influence within you, and it is up to you to own it and decide what you are going to do with it from where you stand today.

Remember you have the power to be a person of influence and make a difference. Remember that. You can lead wherever you are, but leadership will never be a title or rank. It will always be influence. The opportunities are endless for you. Don't limit yourself based on your circumstances. You are called for more, you are called to influence. . . . you are a leader!

---

13 Lois Melkonian, "The secret behind how to influence people," *BetterUp*, 13 January 2021, https://www.betterup.com/blog/the-secret-behind-how-to-influence-people.

CHAPTER 2

YOUR WHY

Why?
Why?
Why?

This is a question I have asked so many times and I am sure you have, too.

What is your why? Why is it important to know your why? Why is knowing your why relevant? This chapter will answer these questions. Mark Twain once said, "The two most important days in your life are the day you are born and the day you find out why."[14] To discover your why, ask yourself, "Why do I get out of bed in the morning?" Why do you do what you do and why should anyone care? These are tough questions that take great intentionality and self-reflection to answer.

We all know the WHAT and HOW in what we do, but once we try and explain our purpose, things get difficult. In *Start with Why*, Simon Sinek "shows us that our 'why' is actually the heart of everything we do, and that understanding it is the key to both

---

14 Mark Twain, "The two most important days in your life are the day you are born and the day you find out why," quoted in "Start with Why: The Importance of Finding Your Purpose," *REVBY*, 15 December 2020, https://www.revby.co/post/start-with-why.

feeling fulfilled in your own life and inspiring others.[15] Your why allows you to connect to the deepest part of yourself and makes you hone in on the ways God has made you unique. Proverbs 19:21 states, "Many are the plans in a person's heart, but it is the LORD's purpose that prevails." You may have a lot of dreams, aspirations, and goals in life, but think about what is driving all of that. Do they carry your calling and uniqueness? In the previous chapter, there was a lot of discussion on influence and leadership. You are a person of influence, but to be an effective person of influence and an effective leader, it is foundational to start with your why.

MY WHY

I'll start with my why—the journey of finding it and how it evolved over time.

YOUR WHY IS NOT WHAT YOU DO.

I did not realize that my why extended beyond my WHAT. I thought my WHY for pursuing a career in aviation was just that—because I wanted a career in aviation. However, I realized that was incorrect once I started my first job in the aviation industry. I assumed my WHY was to become an airline pilot growing up near the great San Francisco International Airport. I quickly

---

15 Simon Sinek, *Start With Why: How Great Leaders Inspire Everyone to Take Action* (Portfolio, December 27, 2011), quoted in Angie Harms, "The Power of Starting with 'Why,'" *ibtm*, 26 July 2022, https://ibtmevents.com/blog/career-development/power-of-starting-with-why/.

realized that would not be possible due to the exorbitant costs of flight training during my time at university. From the start, I had mixed my why with my what. Your why is not what you do. Your why is based on your purpose beyond the what.

When I started my first job in the aviation industry, I fell in love with being around private jets and I loved meeting new people every day and serving whomever I encountered, including my co-workers. I enjoyed what the company stood for and the possible growth opportunities. I thought I had found my new WHY, which is to pursue growth in the private jet niche of aviation. Again, I mixed the why and the what. I found out later on that there was more to life than my career.

I became fully immersed in this side of the aviation field and invested in the company I was working for at the time. I only lived a few minutes from work, and I would work as much as I could, not for the money—but because I had found my WHY—or so I thought.

After working a few years in front-line roles, I was promoted to my first leadership role. I knew nothing about leadership or how to lead. The only thing I knew was that as a new leader, I wanted to look after my people and mentor them just like leaders had done for me in the past. Those leaders cared for me and my growth. I wanted to do the same for the people I led. I needed to learn more about this leadership thing, so I pursued my doctorate in executive leadership at the University of Charleston. Going through this program broadened my horizons and helped me grow tremendously as a leader.

I remember during my first residency in the doctorate program, the instructors asked the students to each write all of the roles we played on rocks with an adjective in front of them. I had a dedicated leader, open learner, helpful mentor, and involved church member. After this, we then used our rocks to help form our personal mission statement. My mission statement is a bit lengthy because I put my all into this exercise and it was at that point in my life that I realized there is more to my life than WHAT I was doing, which was my aviation career. My life had more meaning than that, and it was in this exercise that I truly discovered my WHY.

Here is my personal mission statement that I put together during my first residency at the University of Charleston:

A young, diversified individual whose purpose is to follow Christ and continue to accomplish for His glory. To continue to persevere through obstacles and challenges that may come about in his aspirations. To be a dedicated leader and develop individuals to desire to become effective leaders. An open learner continually developing himself to attain higher education to mentor others just like those who helped him attain success and satisfaction in his career. A helpful mentor who enjoys networking with younger students and leading them in the right direction to make the appropriate decisions in life that will help them achieve success. A man who continues to be an involved church member, engaged in the congregation and spreading the good Word. An enthusiastic community member that finds new and innovative ways to help those where he lives and works. A caring son who enjoys spending time with his parents, being someone they can count on, and seeking advice to shape his life decisions for the better. A person who would like to impact people's lives and point them in the appropriate direction to achieve the success he has thus far. He aspires to complete the DEL Program at the University of Charleston to become a professor and mentor students. He strives to attain an upper-level managerial role within the organization he currently works for to develop frontline team members toward managerial roles. Most importantly, he continues to focus on his faith, and it is only by God's grace that he continues to be a driven, accomplished individual.

The school laminated the statement for us and made several copies for us to keep. I then put this up in my bedroom and on my desk at home, so I always remembered my WHY summed up in the personal mission statement I developed at the start of the doctorate program. I realized that there is more to life than just a career or job. I had other ways of living out my purpose and calling and it was more than just the career I was pursuing.

Developing my mission statement helped center me as I shifted my focus to not only continue my career journey but also better myself in being a brother, a son, and a mentor, and also outline my goals at the time. You will note in the personal mission statement that I aim to complete the doctorate program and become an upper-level manager and professor someday, all of which I am still pursuing today. This exercise helped me develop what I would call my WHY and my "North Star."

FIND YOUR WHY

Life does a great job of keeping us distracted and focused only on the moment we are in. We go through our days going to work, coming home, and running errands without thinking about much of anything else.

In a Forbes article, Paula Black writes that "we are built to do so much more than simply survive; we are built to thrive and build a life that we love, not just make a living."[16] Paula further expands that finding your North Star helps you live with purpose and gives you that reference point to keep you moving in the right direction. My North Star came from writing out my personal mission statement.

> **BE CONTENT WITH YOUR PROGRESS, KNOWING THAT YOU'RE ONE STEP CLOSER TO YOUR MISSION.**

It was a very challenging exercise to go through because I had placed my why in my career. To discover your why, it may be useful to complete an exercise similar to mine that outlines all the roles in your life and all the things you do. Take some time to reflect on how you are doing in each of those roles, and then outline your goals for all that you do and who you want to become.

Don't get too caught up on your goals. Writing your goals is important, however, there is more to it—understanding and determining your overall purpose, or your North Star. The purpose of your North Star is to help you make informed decisions

---

[16] Paula Black, "Live With Purpose: How to Find Your 'North Star,'" *Forbes*, 12 November 2019, https://www.forbes.com/sites/forbescoachescouncil/2019/11/12/live-with-purpose-how-to-find-your-north-star/?sh=49d8f7405fa1.

today. Be content with your progress, knowing that you're one step closer to your mission.

Successful businessman and entrepreneur, Gary Vaynerchuk, aspires to become the owner of the New York Jets, a lifelong dream that holds significant importance to him. His daily endeavors are focused on achieving this specific objective. Whether it involves forming new partnerships, making personnel changes, or embarking on fresh ventures, his guiding principle and goal—his North Star—influences all of his choices.[17] Finding your why may help you get unstuck and find an anchor in your life. In his book *Your Purpose Is Calling*, Dr. Dharius Daniels writes that carrying out your calling and purpose isn't simply doing something, but becoming someone.[18]

What do you do when you are feeling stuck? You may be reading this chapter and having difficulty even thinking about your why. Your mind may be running at your fastest speed ever, and you may even feel anxious. In *Living With Purpose*, Michelle Hubert identifies what may keep us stuck and hold us back:

- Living according to someone else's values
- Comparing ourselves to others
- Making decisions based on fear
- Relying on someone else to develop us or drive our growth[19]

If you are struggling with any of these or feel stuck, you need to hone in and cherish your own uniqueness. God created you with a purpose and intent and He made you unique. I remember early

---

17 Gary Vaynerchuk, "Why I Want to Buy the NY Jets," Filmed 16 Sept. 2016 at Larry King Now, YouTube, https://www.youtube.com/watch?v=ITs7KzUPPuQ.
18 Dr. Dharius Daniels, *Your Purpose Is Calling: Your Difference Is Your Destiny* (Nashville, TN: Zondervan, September 20, 2022).
19 Michelle Hubert, *Living With Purpose: A Framework for Igniting Your Fullest Potential* (Korsgaden Insights, April 28, 2023).

on when I started working in the aviation industry in college. I felt stuck because I was consistently comparing myself to others, I was listening to what others thought of me, and I wasn't trying to find my own voice. I didn't have a North Star at that time. I had to identify my personal values and what I am good at on my own. What do I enjoy doing? What gives me great happiness? And, as a sneak preview to my final chapter—where do I have the most influence?

I realized that I was very good at helping people and adding value to them, a trait rooted in my upbringing, so I cherished that. I found opportunities in college and in my early years in the aviation industry to help my peers and those around me. I went to work wondering how I could add value to others, and that mindset overflowed not only to my peers but also to customers and clients. I would be very intentional in the relationships that I built with my coworkers. Just as they helped me in training and getting oriented to the job, I added value back in different ways. Frank, my customer service lead and trainer, helped me so much because he introduced me to key customers and caught me up to speed on the job. I would then teach him tricks on the computer and taught him about how to use YouTube—which was huge for him—to add value in return. He is a huge golfer, so he used to watch golf training videos and loved using the platform.

Don't get me wrong, a lot of doubt comes my way, and it will come your way too. You will have many obstacles and great adversity to overcome, but if you stay focused on your why, you will be able to overcome anything. It will pull you out of your what because you will be focused on your higher purpose and your why. You won't let any obstacle get in the way of your why because you are focused on your true purpose in life.

YOUR DIVINE DESIGN IS LIFE HOW GOD INTENDS IT TO BE.

Dr. Kent Ingle, President of Southeastern University, talks a lot about helping people find their divine design. He has a podcast called Framework Leadership and he also takes a deeper dive into his book called *This Adventure Called Life* where he discusses that greatness is more valuable than power, position, or prestige. It's about living a life of significance and meaning. You only discover your greatness when you accept the call to adventure, and you will need to take leaps of faith as you live towards and into your divine design. And this is what ultimately helps set you free and helps you become unstuck.[20]

It starts with honing in on your divine design that will lead you to your why. Your divine design is life how God intends it to be. In this design, there is fullness of life and the glory of God's tangible presence. Once you start discovering your divine design, your why will begin to form. This may take some time and you may have to go through some experiences to eventually find your why. Ephesians 2:10 states "For we are God's handiwork, created in Christ Jesus to do good works, which God prepared

---
[20] Dr. Kent Ingle, *The Adventure Called Life: Discovering Your Divine Design* (Springfield, MO: My Healthy Church, August 1, 2013).

in advance for us to do." God will provide whatever you need to move you in the direction that He called you. He needs you to go through it all—difficult seasons, experiences, obstacles, making mistakes, and failing—to move you in the direction of your why. As Dr. Dharius Daniels mentions, it is your why that will get you through the walls.[21] God will bring you walls for a purpose to help you discover your divine design.

One thing that surprised me is that my why started to change and evolve as life went on. My personal values stayed the same but as I went through different experiences, my why started to slowly shift. I struggled with this greatly because I thought my why would not change, so I was focused on only that why at the time. I realized I longed for more as I progressed through my career in aviation. Something was missing even though I had such a successful career journey of growth. Things started to align over time, and I realized that I needed to do something to help grow leaders and young people. Angie Harms writes,

> Your 'why' can change over the course of time, and you may have more than one 'why' for different activities and aspects of your life, but it is worth taking the time and effort to learn about yourself in this regard. Knowing your 'why'—and keeping an eye on how it changes – is the key to staying passionate about your work, your career, and your life.[22]

I found my greatest fulfillment in helping grow and develop my team members, especially in my early years of leadership. I found great joy in not only training on the technical skills of the

---
21 Daniels, *Your Purpose Is Calling*.
22 Angie Harms, "The Power of Starting with 'Why,'" *ibtm*, 26 July 2022, https://ibtmevents.com/blog/career-development/power-of-starting-with-why/.

job but truly guiding and developing their leadership and giving them the opportunities to thrive and grow. Philippians 2:5-8 really stands out as it pertains to focusing on and helping others. The verses state,

> *In your relationships with one another, have the same mindset as Christ Jesus: Who, being in very nature God, did not consider equality with God something to be used to his own advantage; rather, he made himself nothing by taking the very nature of a servant, being made in human likeness. And being found in appearance as a man, he humbled himself by becoming obedient to death— even death on a cross!*

I learned that Jesus lived his life like a servant with a focus on what He could do for others. I took on that mindset because so many people helped me along my career path and believed that I was called for more, and that is why my why ends with serving others.

This also takes me back to Pastor Craig Groeschel's sermon titled "Find Your Way." In it, he talks about the story of David and Saul. David wasn't trying to find his purpose by running for his life from Saul; David was trying to fulfill God's purpose. David wasn't pursuing his dream; he was pursuing God's purpose. David wasn't seeking a position; he was serving a purpose. Pastor Craig mentioned, "If you want to serve God's purpose, start serving God's people."[23] Scan the QR code to watch this sermon (I highly recommend it!).

---

23 Pastor Craig Groeschel, "Find Your Why," Filmed 25 Apr. 2020, *YouTube*, https://www.youtube.com/watch?v=jWYbHNBTFng.

Start with the servant mindset and serve people. Value people just like Jesus did when he walked the earth.

REMEMBER YOUR WHY

I noticed I sometimes lost sight of my why, purpose, calling, and the divine design that God has called me to fulfill. I began to lose sight of my identity. As I started to have what I could call "wins" at work through promotion after promotion, I lost sight of my why and the reason why I wanted to pursue leadership in the first place. I was longing for the next win where I would find my validation. It didn't change the way I led as a leader, but my mindset and inner voice did. My why shifted to looking for the next win, looking for the next opportunity where I could stand out in the company, looking for the next opportunity for recognition, and looking for the "pat on the back." I was privileged to experience several leadership roles at a young age, and through this, I started to define myself and put my identity in the WHAT and lost sight of my WHY. I was traveling for the company I worked for at the time and was getting so much exposure to company executives and industry leaders. Jordan Montgomery mentioned in episode 109 of *The Leadership Download Podcast*, "I was overexposed and underdeveloped."[24] I felt like I was on "cloud nine," but then I started to feel a sense of emptiness from success. There were times when I lost sight of my faith, my family, and my friends, and I became very selfish. My successes and opportunities for more success and validation drove everything I did. In my first book, *Navigation and Discovery*, I discuss how this negatively impacted my life as I defined myself by my WHAT instead of my

---
24 Montgomery, "The Journey of Success in Your Youth."

WHY. Burnout was one of the effects, and I burned out badly.[25] Jon Gordon mentions that we don't get burned out because of what we do, we get burned out because we forget why we do it.[26] And this is what happened to me. I truly lost sight of my why.

> **I WANTED TO BE A LEADER WHO TRULY LOOKS AFTER HIS PEOPLE AND IS INVESTED IN THEIR LIVES BEYOND WORK.**

It wasn't until living abroad in the Caribbean on the twin island of Antigua and Barbuda that I truly got back to defining myself based on my WHY. I began to learn that there's more to life than just my career. There is faith, family, and friends, and also diversifying myself with more hobbies, personal growth, and having fun and living life to the fullest. I started to play golf again, learn more about leadership, spend more time calling family, and spend more time with friends.

Early on in my front-line roles, I encountered both good and bad leaders; however, no leader is perfect, and I learned a lot from them. I wanted to be a leader who truly looks after his people and is invested in their lives beyond work. This stems from my Christian faith in sharing God's love with others—loving people just as God loves us. This began to overflow into the rest of my

---
25 Singh, *Navigation and Discovery.*
26 Jon Gordon, X post, Oct. 30, 2022, 9:05 pm, https://x.com/JonGordon11/status/1586887142541733888.

life as I wanted to be more like Jesus who just loves and values people—and that is all. I tried so hard to focus on my why for a well-rounded life. Once I refocused on my why, it changed over time and my divine design evolved.

As I moved towards learning more about leadership through the doctorate program, I realized that I wanted to help young people strive for higher. Many of those whom I grew up with limited themselves based on their circumstances and upbringing. I stopped seeking and longing for the next success, and I became focused on helping others, which, by the way, is my WHY for writing this book and my first book, *Navigation and Discovery*.

Over time you may find that your why and divine design will evolve as you evolve. That's completely fine. You may experience something that pushes you in a different direction, and that is completely okay as long as you cherish that change. You may also reach your goal, which means it's time to set a new goal. This could mean an extension of your current goal or a new one altogether.

Your why is going to drive your purpose and is key to staying grounded and focused on that North Star. As Martindale Brightwood mentions in her TEDx Talk, "Your why can take you on a negative or a positive journey, it's up to you to choose."[27] What a true statement, because you will face adversity and obstacles, and there will be times when you feel like quitting, so you have to remember your why.

Nathan Harmon states, "If you have a good why, no matter what happens you will not quit because quitting is not an option because you have a why, you have a passion, and you have a

---

27 Martindale Brightwood, "Remember Your Way & Live In Your Purpose," Filmed 14 June 2021, *YouTube*, https://www.youtube.com/watch?v=0ZgZjKyRTiU.

purpose. You're on a mission to achieve something and nothing can knock you off course!"[28]

THERE MAY BE TIMES THAT YOU WILL FACE RESISTANCE AS YOU BEGIN TO DREAM BIG.

Sometimes the easiest thing to do is quit. It is my faith in God that has helped me stay the course during the times when I hit rock bottom and faced adversity. My faith has helped me go through those times and seasons of adversity and I've learned to face the many challenges and obstacles head-on, as I know there is always more adversity to come. There may be times that you will face resistance as you begin to dream big. People will put you down and say you will never become who you hope to become, never achieve that dream, or never achieve success. Don't live your life based on the expectations and voices of others. Hone in and cherish the divine design that God has called you to live out via your purpose and calling. As novelist Fyodor Dostoyevsky wrote, "The mystery of human existence lies not in just staying alive, but in finding something to live for."[29]

Start with building your personal mission statement. This may take some time. Write out all the areas of your life that you have

---

28 Nathan Harmon, "When You Feel Like Quitting: Remember Your Why!—Powerful Motivational Video," Filmed September 9, 2020, *YouTube*, https://www.youtube.com/watch?v=xPxhyY9xTZs.
29 Fyodor Dostoyevsky, *The Brothers Karamazov* (New York, NY: Farrar, Straus and Giroux, June 14, 2002), 306-307.

influence in. Evaluate each of the areas and assess where you are today and where you want to take yourself. It won't be an easy task. Post it somewhere where you will see it every day— your bathroom mirror, your desk at home, or your desk at the office— to remind yourself of your why. We have talked about influence and your why. Let's dive into leadership and what I learned from my early years of leadership. I learned the most through making mistakes, facing failure after failure, and being a young leader who was unprepared to take on leadership. I hope that through my journey, you will learn it is okay to fail, and you will find your way through. Whether you are a student, aspiring leader, young leader, or new leader, I hope the rest of this book is a blessing to your life and leadership.

CHAPTER 3
PEOPLE, PRODUCT, PROCESS

People, Product, Process.

This is a huge leadership principle I learned early on as I stepped into leadership roles in the aviation industry. Through my mentor, Pasquale, I was introduced to a show on CNBC called *The Profit*, hosted by Marcus Lemonis. In *The Profit*, Marcus invests in small, struggling businesses to help turn them around. However, his investment was not the key to success or transformation. The episodes would start first with Marcus acquainting himself with the people who own and work for the business. First, he focuses solely on the people to understand the foundation of the business. Then, he learns the business's processes and the products and services they offer. He first sought to resolve issues with the people before he touched the processes and products of the business. I learned so much about leadership watching this show, but I also realized I emulated these practices early in my leadership journey. First, let's look at the 3 Ps Marcus developed: People, Process, Product, also known as PPP.

> **YOU CAN GET SO CAUGHT UP IN THE BUSINESS AND ADMINISTRATIVE ELEMENTS OF LEADERSHIP THAT YOU START TO LOSE SIGHT OF THE PEOPLE YOU LEAD.**

The People, Process, Product (PPP) framework is a business improvement approach. The framework helps businesses identify opportunities for improvement and develop strategies to maximize performance. It also helps business owners and leaders focus on the many moving parts of their business with a systems mindset. The 3Ps are often called the cornerstone of everything a business does. They provide the highest return for a business's efforts. Marcus Lemonis believes that people are the most important of the three Ps. Without good people, good processes and good products only do so much. He states, "The customer is not No. 1 to me. They're No. 2, right behind the employee."[30]

Learning about this principle transformed my leadership because you can get so caught up in the business and administrative elements of leadership that you start to lose sight of the people you lead. I experienced this several times and found that this is a trickle-down effect. When you don't have the right people, you don't have the right processes, you deliver a poor product/service.

---

[30] *The Profit*, Amber Mazzola (July 30, 2013; Englewood Cliffs, NJ: CNBC), Television.

PEOPLE

It is the people that form the foundation of any business, and the key to having good people is having them in a thriving environment. One element of people is having them in the right roles where they can grow and develop. Marcus Lemonis mentions, "Businesses are based on relationships and relationships are based on people," says Marcus, "So, surround yourself with good people."[31]

I learned early on in my aviation career that having a successful business starts with the people. People are the heart of any organization. An organization thrives when people are supported, heard, and feel a sense of belonging that they are a part of something bigger. In leadership, when we talk about people, we must think long-term, and we have to master our interpersonal skills.

I was promoted to be a leader on a startup team for a brand-new location with the company I was working for at the time. The company had never done this before, so I was tasked with a lot, though I had the freedom of execution. It involved the onboarding of new team members and training them to set up and prepare the location for success to be ready on opening day. I realized that this was a rare opportunity as we had the chance to build a team culture and an organizational culture from scratch. Usually, new leaders come into organizations or teams where they have to understand the existing culture and shift as needed, by which Dr. Jon Chasteen coined the term "releader."[32] Here, I had the opportunity to be a part of building something great from scratch. I never knew about the 3Ps principle at the time and

---
31 *The Profit*, Mazzola.
32 Dr Jon Chasteen, *ReLeader: How to Fix What You Didn't Break* (XLeadership, January 16, 2024).

knew very little about leadership. My focus was all on the people we were onboarding and ensuring they felt like they belonged and were being equipped and resourced to perform their jobs once we opened our doors. I remember giving it my all and pouring so much into the team. I went above and beyond our training program to make sure we were going to be the top team and location within the company providing a great product and service. I wanted to make sure they were the most highly trained, and I encouraged the team to ask questions, challenge me, and truly understand the why in every aspect of the job.

Another element was getting to know who they are beyond work. I'll make a disclaimer here: some people open up about their personal lives a lot, and some only open up a little, but in either case, cherish whatever they do choose to share, whether it be their family, their hobbies, or their weekend plans. Then, before you even discuss work, ask them about it the next time you have a conversation with them. My first manager did this; he asked about my school and what I wanted to do in the aviation industry. He asked how I was doing first. He sought after my well-being, and I truly felt I belonged to the team because my leader cared for me. And that is how you keep your people your top priority.

IF YOU DON'T FOCUS ON YOUR PEOPLE, YOU ARE GOING TO FAIL TREMENDOUSLY AS A LEADER.

You must be wondering, "Well that is rare to build a culture from scratch." Yes, it definitely is. Traditionally as a new leader, you will be leading or releading a team or teams with an established culture where you have people. Your initial goals are to get to know your team and understand who they are beyond work. One thing I did when leading a new team was meet with each team member privately. I learned this from my mentor Pasquale who was promoted to lead at a different location that came with great challenges. To integrate himself into the team and understand the culture, he met with everyone privately to truly understand the people and the culture. I found this so valuable as I got to understand each team member and gain an understanding of the culture. Through witnessing his process, I learned the pain points of the team and got a pulse on the culture. Spending time with your people is key to winning them over. If you don't focus on your people, you are going to fail tremendously as a leader. I have seen leaders get caught up in the business activities of their job and general administrative busyness which limited their time with the team. You have to understand that the people you lead are essential and foundational to your business, team, or organization.

PROCESS

Process is the next P of the 3Ps. Process is next because your people need to work as efficiently and productively as possible. You want to look at your operational processes carefully to understand every step from receiving an order to delivering the finished product or service. As Marcus says, "Control your cash, stick to your core business, and know your numbers."[33] Ultimately, process refers to the different systems you need in your business to achieve a consistent outcome.

Systems are crucial to your business's success because they ensure things are replicated in a positive way. Once you have a system for each area in your business, you'll need to document it so that everyone is crystal clear on how it works, how to do the task, and what the expectations are. When it's documented, it can be followed—and measured and tweaked if need be. With this also comes accountability. Our job as leaders is to first make sure that we are providing the right tools and resources to equip them to perform their jobs with great success. If we are doing that, and people can't perform, then we need to hold them accountable. We can't hold people accountable if we are not equipping them properly.

In *The Profit*, I have seen in many of the episodes that the processes often limit or prohibit the success of the business whether it be because everything has to go through the boss or that several inefficiencies reduce the output of the business.

When I was building the startup team, I wanted to make sure that the team—not me or other leaders—drove the processes. I wanted to have our team's fingerprints on everything once we opened our doors so that they felt they were part of the true startup and not just the worker bees so they would take more pride in their work. We took feedback from the team, refined it, and tried it out. If it didn't work, we refined it again until it did work, not only for the sake of our team but also to deliver a good product and service. Simplicity helped in this case. Keeping things

---

[33] *The Profit*, Mazzola.

simple is sometimes the best way to go. I've experienced leaders complicating the processes so much that the output of the product or service becomes degraded.

I learned so much from Niall and Pasquale under their close mentorship and from leading several teams and organizations. I liked the process training I received from Niall because it was remarkably difficult to lead a team that was so spread out across several sites in one airport. There were significant challenges with communication. Niall had implemented several processes using technology to enable his team to be efficient and productive. The processes that were implemented did not take much time; however, they made our leadership team more cohesive and well-informed of our entire operation. As we evolved, the processes needed to evolve as well, and that's important to remember. You can change the processes at any time as long as it helps your people work more efficiently and serves your clients or customers more effectively.

If you are a new leader or have stepped into leading a new team or department, you must look at your processes and ask your team for feedback to help refine them so that you can deliver a better product and service. I remember in my first senior leadership role; I was leading a team where the processes all involved the leader. The previous leader that I succeeded had all processes go through their desk, and that overwhelmed me. I quickly realized that the people were not being equipped or developed. I had to shift my focus to the people and focus on their growth and development and give them opportunities to thrive. Doing so eliminated several processes. I instantly saw team members more engaged in the business because I had given them more autonomy and decision-making privileges over issues closest to the operation that truly mattered.

So, take a look at your processes wherever you are within your organization or team and find ways to help better your team so that you can deliver better products and services.

PRODUCT

Product is the final P of the 3Ps because if you have the right people on your team in the right place with the right processes, you can deliver the right product and service. You want to have products and services that meet the needs of your market. Whether you serve consumers or businesses, your business needs to offer the right products for your customers. As Marcus says, your product line and services should be practical, purposeful, and profitable.

In some of *The Profit* episodes, you see many businesses develop their products without listening to customer feedback or they develop products that do not sell because they don't meet the needs of the market. Many leaders fail to solicit feedback from their team on the products and services. Marcus emphasizes the importance of a strong product line that can open the door to new business opportunities. I observed Marcus help business owners refine their products to only a few that they thrive at the most, which allows scalability.[34]

I saw myself living out this final P even when I was a front-line employee. I always tried to find ways to deliver our products and services more effectively. How can we take it to another level? Is there something new we can offer? Starting as a front-line

---

34 *The Profit*, Mazzola.

employee, I practiced listening to our customers and continued to carry this skill forward throughout my leadership journey.

On the startup team that I mentioned earlier, we had the basic products and services that were the core of our business, but we took it to a whole new level. We developed the company's first customer appreciation program where we started to develop loyal customers; however, this only started after we learned how to execute our basic products and services flawlessly. To take your products and services to a new level, your team must execute them with confidence to build trust with your customers. Once you build and establish that trust, it's time to take things to a new level. We started to improve and enhance our amenities and customer experience to leave a more memorable and lasting impression. We started to shift our focus to relationship building because we continued to stay focused on executing the basics flawlessly. Our team members were able to do the same and focus on relationship-building with our customers which ultimately helped us to deliver a great product and service.

Through Niall and Pasquale, who were running the company's most profitable locations and delivering a high-level product and service, I learned that delivering the basic product and services with high quality consistently was very difficult because of the size of the locations. To do it, we went backward and refined our processes, but we had to start with our people. At times, we had to hold our people accountable or equip them with more resources. Then, we revised some of our processes, removing old ones and implementing new ones. There may be times when you have to work backward when a service failure or a product mishap happens. Take a look at the Ps and evaluate where you need to assess, evaluate, and refine. Once you master applying the 3Ps to your leadership, the opportunities are endless. The 3P process will also help you define your own style. Though I never tried to be like them, I learned from so many great leaders, including Niall and Pasquale. I took their best traits and created my own unique leadership style. In the next chapter, we will take a deeper dive into discovering your personality and how it translates to your leadership style.

CHAPTER 4

DEFINING YOUR LEADERSHIP STYLE AND PATH

Understanding and defining your own leadership style is a journey in itself. It took me years to discover my style and find where I am the most comfortable in the way I lead people, and my style is still evolving. I had the privilege of leading different teams across the United States and abroad which enabled me to experience different cultures and environments. I didn't change who I was, but I did have to shift my approach and style based on the environment I was in. Post University mentions, "To be a good leader, you also need to develop a leadership style that suits your skills, the kind of position you have, and the kind of business environment you work in."[35] I am sure you have encountered both good and bad leaders as I have. I have learned from the bad leaders and taken the great traits from the good leaders and created my own style. Sounds easy, doesn't it? Well, there's more to

---
35 Post University, "Develop Your Own Leadership Style to Be an Effective Leader," *Post University Blog*, https://post.edu/blog/develop-your-own-leadership-style-effective-leader/.

it. Developing your own style can help you lead more effectively as you learn to communicate better, understand the needs of your team members, and build good relationships.

IMITATING OTHER LEADERS YOU LOOK UP TO WILL NOT WORK.

First, you have to stop comparing yourself to other leaders or the greatest leaders out there like John Maxwell and Craig Groeschel. Craig Groeschel gave a sermon at the 2016 Hillsong Conference and spoke about running your own race. Yes, you need to run your own race, and playing the comparison game will limit you because you won't grow by comparing. You need to cherish God's unique purpose for you on this earth. Craig Groeschel mentions in the sermon, "The fastest way to kill something special is to compare it to something else."[36]

Imitating the leaders you look up to will not work. Believe me, I tried this early on when I was promoted to my first leadership role. You cannot imitate who you are not. Carey Nieuwhof mentioned in an article, "Learning from other leaders can make you a better leader. Imitating other leaders can do damage." Another thing Carey mentions is that "constant imitation kills innovation" which will put you behind as a leader instead of staying ahead and

---

[36] Craig Groeschel, "Run Your Race: Stop Comparing Yourself to Others," Filmed August 16, 2020 at Transformation Church, *YouTube*, https://www.youtube.com/watch?v=F1pvsXkzy5k.

being creative.[37] When you stay you, you are free to create and further grow as a leader. You also have the opportunity to further yourself beyond the leaders you compare yourselves to. I found myself imitating one of my great mentors whom I met early on in the workforce. I tried to lead like he did, and it did not work at all. I was ineffective because I tried to be like someone else rather than capitalize on my unique approach and style. I didn't even try to find my own style. I didn't develop myself. I just copied someone else. Don't get me wrong, I encourage you to incorporate the traits of leaders you look up to into your own leadership, but ultimately, you need to develop your own style that works for you.

> **IF YOU WANT TO PLEASE JESUS WITH THE WAY YOU LEAD, AND IF YOUR ANSWER IS ANYTHING BESIDES CHRIST, THEN YOU WILL ALWAYS RUN A RACE THAT YOU CANNOT WIN.**

As I mentioned earlier, Craig Groeschel advised to run your own race.[38] Hebrews 12:1-2 states, "Therefore, since we are surrounded by such a great cloud of witnesses, let us throw off everything that hinders and the sin that so easily entangles. And let us run with perseverance the race marked out for us, fixing our eyes on Jesus, the pioneer and perfecter of faith." You are God's

---
37 Carey Nieuwhof, "5 Reasons You Need to Stop Imitating Other Leaders," *Carey Nieuwhof Blog*, https://careynieuwhof.com/5-reasons-you-need-to-stop-imitating-other-leaders/.
38 Groeschel, "Run Your Race."

masterpiece, created by Jesus, to do good works that God prepared for you to do. Imitating others will not lead to any contentment. If you want to please Jesus with the way you lead, and if your answer is anything besides Christ, then you will always run a race that you cannot win. Christ calls us to lead (see 1 Corinthians 12) as one part of the body on behalf of the whole body. Two of the same body parts would make the body inefficient and maybe even unable to function.

You will always feel left behind, left out, and that you can't live up to what you've always hoped to become as a leader.

No two leadership methods are the same. A Harvard Business Review article mentions that developing your own style doesn't start outside the self, it starts from within.[39] You have to be yourself and understand your own natural leadership style. I found authenticity to be a big part of evaluating my leadership. Early on in my leadership, I pretended to be the know-it-all.—I knew everything and had all the answers to everything—yet people saw right through me once I didn't have the answers for something. They lost trust in me. So, I began to focus on being authentic and learning how to use that authenticity and my authority to thrive in my leadership role. I didn't have to pretend like I had the answers to everything. It's okay to not know everything, you just need to know how to get the answers if you don't yet know them.

Sometimes you have to be bold and get out of your comfort zone to lift the lid on your leadership.

I learned how to navigate my own path over time. Don't make the same mistake I did—pave your own path. I tried too hard to

---

[39] Emily Ostermeyer, "4 Tips For Developing Your Personal Leadership Style," *Harvard Business School Online*, 19 Apr. 2019, https://online.hbs.edu/blog/post/developing-your-leadership-style.

take the traditional leadership journey as I moved from one promotion to another up the corporate ladder, but there was a point where I felt stuck. I had to be bold, take risks, set myself apart, and get out of my comfort zone to continue moving forward in my leadership journey. I thought I would be an executive leader for the first company I worked for in the aviation industry because I was tremendously loyal to that company that invested a lot in my development and growth. That didn't happen, and I had to come to terms with that and move on in my leadership journey. Many are uncomfortable with paving their own way, but that's what I did. I remember my colleagues were shocked when I left the company because I had been there for over a decade, but they understood I was on a different trajectory. Sometimes you have to be bold and get out of your comfort zone to lift the lid on your leadership. As John Maxwell mentions, "Leadership ability is the lid that determines a person's level of effectiveness. The lower an individual's ability to lead, the lower the lid on his potential. The higher the individual's ability to lead, the higher the lid on his potential."[40]

Developing your personal brand is one important aspect of leadership. A personal brand is part of your uniqueness. As Harvard Business School mentions, to develop your personal brand and leadership take time out for "self-reflection, understanding the influence of biases, and seeking out opportunities to demonstrate your bravery."[41] Write your own leadership story as I am writing mine. You are unique and there is only one of you. What are you going to do to pave your path? What do you need to shift

---
40 John Maxwell, "The Law of the Lid," *John C Maxwell Blog*, https://www.johnmaxwell.com/blog/the-law-of-the-lid/.
41 Ostermeyer, "4 Tips."

in your leadership to cherish your uniqueness and be yourself? Are you being your true self? Your most authentic self?

Where do you lack authenticity in your workplace?

This all starts with self-awareness. If you don't know yourself, you can't develop or sharpen your leadership skills. Let's start with the basics of self-awareness: your strengths and your weaknesses. What comes naturally to you? Where do you struggle? This may be easy for some and difficult for others. Perhaps you possess exceptional learning abilities and efficiency in completing tasks, although occasionally compromise quality for quantity. Alternatively, you may exhibit confidence in your work yet battle with expressing your thoughts and ideas in conference room discussions. I can relate. I do well in one-on-one conversations, but once you get me in a group setting, I cave, as I find it hard to share in a group setting. What will you do about it? What are you doing now to overcome these obstacles? In my book *Navigation and Discovery*, I wrote a chapter on owning the room and how I gained the confidence to add value to a room or group setting. I had to build the courage to speak and focus on adding value to the group or conversation rather than focus on myself and what others would think of me. I still struggle with this today.

Identifying your strengths and weaknesses through the practice of self-awareness is only the first step, and it's an essential step. The next step is to develop a high level of emotional intelligence. Dr. Travis Bradberry and Jean Greaves, authors of *Emotional Intelligence 2.0*, describe self-awareness as one of the core components of emotional intelligence. They define emotional intelligence as your ability to recognize and understand emotions in yourself and others and your ability to use this awareness to manage your behavior and relationships.[42] Emotional intelligence requires keen attunement to one's surroundings and self-awareness. While we all possess a certain level of empathy towards others' situations and concerns, emotional intelligence becomes particularly crucial in special circumstances. The more you experience different situations and environments, the more you will build a higher level of emotional intelligence. As Tony Robbins mentions,

When faced with problems, true leaders look inward and focus on their own abilities and shortcomings. There are always areas of improvement for leaders. When you ask yourself how you can better empower and inspire your team, you'll naturally discover how to improve your leadership skills—because self-accountability is the foundation of great leadership.[43]

Emotional intelligence helps you make decisions with your people in mind. It helps you to better care for your people. I remember as a front-line employee, I used to resent change because change made our jobs more complicated. To make matters worse, no one told us why the change was being made. When I became a leader, I tried to adopt the mindset of the people I was leading and would ask myself, "How will this change impact the jobs of my team members?" If I could answer that question, I could better explain the reason behind the change and how it would benefit them. If it wouldn't help them, I would explain why the change was important for our organization.

---

42 Dr. Travis Bradberry and Jean Greaves, *Emotional Intelligence 2.0* (TalentSmart, June 13, 2009).
43 Tony Robbins, "Developing Leadership Skills: The Top Areas of Improvement For Leaders and How to Develop Them," *Tony Robbins Blog*, https://www.tonyrobbins.com/leadership-impact/7-ways-to-improve-leadership-skills/.

On one of the episodes of my podcast *Navigation and Discovery with Cameron Singh*, I hosted Richa Awasthi, the former mayor of Foster City, California, and the first Indian woman to be the mayor in that city in over fifty years. She faced a lot of adversity in her journey in politics, but what brought her through was her ability to control her inner voice. She was self-aware of her thoughts, and she stopped them immediately if they were negative. This practice helped her achieve her goal of becoming mayor.[44]

I first learned about the DiSC assessment at the start of the doctorate program at the University of Charleston. It helped me become more self-aware. The DiSC measures your personality traits to help understand behavior in the workplace. The results were so accurate. I've taken many personality assessments before, but the DiSC was the most accurate. It has been long recognized as a great foundation for building leadership skills and provides powerful insights on how you can improve and adapt to other styles.

I offer an individual DiSC assessment with a coaching call. You can find the DiSC Assessment on my website (see Appendix).

Lead the way that feels right. This is such a valuable lesson in learning how to lead. I once hosted Fraser Grant on my podcast, and he talked about being all in in whatever you do, especially in leadership.[45] You can't cut corners in leadership. You have to be all in with your team in taking them to the next level. The fun stuff starts when you are all in. During my time in the Caribbean,

---

[44] Richa Awasthi, "Breaking the Glass Ceiling," June 2023, in *Navigation and Discovery with Cameron Singh*, podcast, episode 10, https://open.spotify.com/episode/5HnD248b00yhYODxFnLB3U?si=41f803df5dfe40b5.

[45] Fraser Grant, "Going Against the Norms to Achieve Financial and Life Freedom," *Navigation and Discovery with Cameron Singh*, podcast, August 2023, episode 13, https://open.spotify.com/episode/3GUUZsz5NgesvvU2b7wgpW?si=ee574970f6044dfe.

I had just started to get to know the team and understand the culture. I realized the team was anxious about having a young leader. They were uncertain of what was to come, so I set up an initial team meeting. I ended up writing a vision statement for our team which was well received, and it allowed them to see where I saw us heading in the future and gave them clarity on what to expect. This was not something the company told us to do; I did it simply because it felt right. This decision stemmed from the mission statement exercise that I did in my first residency of the doctorate program. Develop your leadership philosophy and vision and do what you feel is right.

YOU CAN'T CUT CORNERS IN LEADERSHIP.

When you do what you know is right, you will inspire others. You are there to inspire your team to work harder and reach greater heights. A huge part of developing your style is to develop your team and push them to the next level.

A lot of this has to do with more than just your WHY. It's about finding your higher purpose. You must know why you're putting time and effort into your chosen goal as a leader. What drives you?

Do you do what you do because you want to help others? I love to help and pour into others, a proclivity that is rooted in my Christian faith. Philippians 2:3 states, "Do nothing out of selfish ambition or vain conceit. Rather, in humility value others above yourselves." I've always aimed to practice this in the workplace, even in my front-line roles.

Seeking feedback is another practice that can help to develop your own leadership style. I always sought feedback from my team, my boss, and other leaders both after meetings and to garner some general reflections on how things were going. I used every opportunity to seek feedback because I wanted to be a better leader for my team and to do that, I needed to take criticism—both bad and constructive. There are several ways to gather feedback, but ultimately, it should always help you gain a different perspective and challenge your assumptions and biases. Seeking feedback will help you broaden your horizons and improve your leadership.

I have also sought mentorship since college. Mentorship became a big part of my life as I started to explore different career paths and opportunities within the aviation industry. On my podcast, Pastor David Lindell of James River Church discussed mentorship and not overlooking those around him for guidance.[46] Seek mentorship and lean into those relationships. Who's the mentor in your own backyard? I sought mentorship from my professors, faith leaders, and peers within the company, and wise mentorship from those well ahead of me. Seeking mentorship allows you to learn from others outside of your normal circles. Curiosity never ends as I continue to seek mentorship. I always like to ask questions, test different scenarios, and receive new ideas on how to enhance my leadership. Wise mentorship has played a huge part in the evolution of my leadership style.

---

46 Pastor David Lindell, "The Path of Purpose: Navigating Life and Leadership," *Navigation and Discovery with Cameron Singh*, podcast, episode 14, https://open.spotify.com/episode/5ulupslUiFcNHvJlqrTCvj?si=fda47de2366f47b2.

There are also times in leadership when you simply have to trust your gut. In an interview with astronaut Sara Sabry on my podcast, she talked about how she had to trust her gut in pursuing her goal of becoming an astronaut. She shared that she had to follow her own ideas and not let other people's voices and opinions limit her abilities. She trusted her gut and kept focused on the goal of becoming an astronaut and she became the first Egyptian, African, and Arab woman to launch into space on Blue Origin's New Shepard rocket.[47] Like Sara, there were many times I had to trust my gut. When the opportunity came to move abroad and live in the Caribbean, I was so nervous. I took very little counsel. I talked to my family and as always, they were supportive, but I knew they were nervous as well. I trusted my gut and accepted the opportunity because I knew it was a once-in-a-lifetime opportunity, and it was the most memorable time of my life so far. I followed my gut when it was time to leave the company I had been working for for over a decade. Follow your gut even when other voices and your inner voices tell you no. You never know what opportunities may come your way. Saying yes required leaning on my faith. I put all my trust in God knowing that my future was in his hands, as Jeremiah 29:11 says.

Your leadership journey can take you anywhere. It can take you places where you never thought you would be. As I mentioned earlier, I tried to follow the traditional path of climbing the corporate ladder, but I got stuck because I knew that I was destined for more. Climbing the corporate ladder would have limited me and my growth. I trusted my gut to make a change and I never

---
47 Sara Sabry, "Journey to Space Exploration," *Navigation and Discovery with Cameron Singh*, podcast, episode 7, https://open.spotify.com/episode/2HqsLxL59DA9tiDFWTyiSt?si=1dcaa95d1ec54516.

looked back. Many thought I was putting too much on myself in pursuing a doctorate, but I did it anyway because that was a dream of mine. Do things that feel right for you and your leadership journey. I am thankful to have had God by my side even during times when I didn't feel Him. My faith is what helped get me through the uncertainty and yes, a lot of uncertainty was behind each opportunity, from moving out of the house, to New Jersey, to living abroad in the Caribbean, to leaving the company I loved so dearly and had invested in for over a decade, to relocating to Colorado and now to Southern California. Next, we will discuss being bold, taking risks, getting out of your comfort zone, and setting yourself apart. All four of these practices helped to define my style and paved the way for my leadership journey. Of course, this did not come easy, but I will share how I navigated through discomfort in order to take my leadership to the next level.

Pave your own path toward where you feel God has called you in the sphere you aspire to grow.

CHAPTER 5

TAKE RISKS

I did not realize that taking risks would help me move forward in life as much as it has. I did not realize that it would open up so many opportunities for me. In his book *You Can Live the Dream*, Nick Nilson writes, "I wonder how many times we see closed doors around the things God has for us, and instead of walking toward those doors, we turn around and walk away."[48] Reflect and think back on how many times you were too fearful to walk through the open doors to see what was on the other side. Nick talks about fear and encourages people to go forth and do it afraid. All it takes is that one step and that one risk to change the trajectory of not only your life but also the people around you.

Sometimes that first step into the unknown takes a lot out of you. You may be thinking of some opportunities that have come up in the past that you probably should have taken, but fear may have limited you. In his book *Defy the Odds,* Pastor Benny Tate mentions that fear truly can steal your future.[49] That is so true.

---
48 Nick Nilson, *You Can Live the Dream: Trading Disappointment and Discontentment for Peace, Joy, and Fulfillment* (Nashville, TN: FaithWords, August 8, 2023).
49 Benny Tate, *Defy the Odds: How God Can Use Your Past to Shape Your Future* (Eugene, OR: Harvest House Publishers, March 8, 2022).

Many opportunities have come my way, but I was too fearful to take the leap of faith and give it a go.

SOMETIMES YOU HAVE TO TRY AND THEN FAIL.

Within this chapter, I will show you through my experiences how taking risks boldly brought forth opportunities that allowed me to step into leadership roles at a very young age. I learned a great deal through these experiences. I know taking risks is easier said than done, but the reality is that some risks may not work in your favor. This is where you have to fail forward. Sometimes you have to try and then fail. That is okay and a part of your growth. Believe me, I have failed more than you know, but I failed forward and learned from them for the next time. 1 Corinthians 10:13 (NKJV) states,

> No temptation has overtaken you except such as is common to man; but God is *faithful*, who will not allow you to be tempted beyond what you are able, but with the temptation will also make the way *of escape, that you may be able to bear* it.

Paul is saying that failure is inevitable but that you can get through it in God's strength. I will unpack this a bit more in the next chapter.

Elon Musk once said, "It gets harder to do things that might not work out. So now is the time to do that. Before you have those obligations. So, I would encourage you to take risks now, and to do something bold. You won't regret it."[50] For me, taking risks and being bold started when I realized I was not very good at advanced courses in high school and instead took evening and online community college classes to get ahead and start earning college credits. It wasn't easy because I had to balance high school and community college. I was afraid I would continue to fail and take on too much. Many of my peers thought I was crazy trying to take on such a large course load, but I loved these courses, as I got the chance to interact with people older than me. The work wasn't easy, and I had to put extra effort and time into the coursework to make sure I got good grades. Taking the risk enabled me to graduate San Jose State University in a little over two years because by the time I graduated high school, I had completed around two years worth of college credits. I was fearful throughout the entire time that I took the college courses—primarily the fear of failure—but I continued to press forward, persevere, and give it my all.

THAT WAS THE FIRST TIME I REALIZED THAT BOLDNESS IS WELL WORTH THE RISK.

---

[50] Elon Musk, "It gets harder to do things... You won't regret it," *USC Marshall School of Business speech*, quoted in "'Take risks now and to do something bold': Elon Musk," *The Indian Express*, 18 June 2021, https://indianexpress.com/article/lifestyle/life-positive/take-risks-now-and-to-do-something-bold-elon-musk-7363566/.

I also developed my boldness when I decided to pursue an aviation career. Becoming an airline pilot was a lifelong dream of mine, and I was able to solidify this career path in high school by taking a college career prep class, AVID. Other people wanted me to pursue the medical field but I had no desire to do that. I feared even stepping into a clinic or onto a hospital campus because of the various health challenges I had growing up. Boldly, I stuck to aviation and eventually went to study aviation at San Jose State University.

After finalizing all my plans for college, I was so proud of myself for pursuing something that I was so passionate about. That was the first time I realized that boldness is well worth the risk. I continued college and took small steps of boldness by getting involved in industry networking groups, talking to other aviation professionals, and getting my questions answered about the many opportunities in the aviation field. Ultimately, networking is how I found my first job in aviation. I was so afraid of networking as such a reserved and timid person. The idea rattled me. I pushed myself every month to attend these networking events, and my professors started to introduce me to people. Eventually, I became more comfortable in meeting new people and other professionals in the industry.

I took another risk after college when I tried to become a professor. My aviation professors and the passion they had for the students inspired me so much. I voiced my interest in teaching, so one of my professors, Glynn Falcon, took a leap of faith and allowed me to substitute for his courses while he completed his work as an attorney, which was his primary job. I loved every part of being a professor. Becoming a professor is my ultimate goal—it's the whole reason I pursued a doctorate and I am so excited to say that I am now an aviation professor in Southern California. I knew it wasn't going to be an easy journey. I was already so tired of school after I completed graduate school, but I went for it anyway, keeping my goal in the forefront of my mind: not only would a doctorate give me a professorship, but it would also open up other great opportunities for me in the future.

Even when I started my first job in the aviation industry in front-line roles, I had to be bold and provide feedback to my managers. Slowly, over time, I became less afraid to speak up. Through this process, I earned great credibility from my managers, and they often sought guidance from me and asked for my feedback because I had earned their trust. It also became easier over time to provide feedback. I didn't want to be *too* bold, so I took a methodical and purposeful approach and focused on where I could add value because I wanted to grow within the company and be on the path to leadership.

I was so eager to grow that I took another big risk. When I first started with the company, I was sent on travel to attend national and regional industry events where I learned a lot more about the aviation industry and company I was with at the time. I got more exposure to leaders from all over the country and networked on a broader scale with people from different parts of the world. This was not easy because I had to represent the company I worked for at the time. I enjoyed the exposure at these events and the opportunity to meet and interact with company executives and corporate team members within the U.S. and across the globe. It was very intimidating to be around the executives until I began to voice my intentions and growth goals! Once I did, they circled around me and helped me move in the right direction towards growth and further development. The exposure made me feel uneasy at first, but I was able to build confidence over time and became more comfortable interacting with industry leaders and those in high positions.

One year, I wasn't invited to attend a national industry event called NBAA Business Aviation Convention and Exhibition. There were a lot of budget cuts so they limited travel and who could travel. Instead, I took vacation time and paid out of my pocket to travel to the event. The company had more tickets to the event but was limited in travel costs. I showed up and got great exposure again with the company, but this time was different. Since I was not attending on the company dime, I took advantage of networking with other companies and attending sessions that I had never had the opportunity to do before. I would pop over to our company booth periodically to say hello to everyone. Eric, my long-time mentor, introduced me to Michael, the CEO of our parent company, and mentioned that I was looking to grow and find other leadership opportunities. Michael and I chatted a bit, and then he mentioned an opportunity in San Francisco with our sister company with the support provided to the airlines. He suggested I connect with him after the event. I called his assistant the following week.

After about twenty or thirty phone calls and one month later, I finally got to speak with him. The opportunity he presented appealed to me—they needed a lot of help, but I didn't need to relocate to help them. The position was at the same airport where I already worked, just not in the private jet sector. I was introduced to my new manager, Steve who wrote the foreword for this book, and a few months later, I landed my first leadership role at the age of twenty-two—responsible for over 200 employees.

Talk about a risk! Regardless, I was so eager for growth that I had to try. Several people discouraged me from trying to pursue the growth opportunity, but I did not take their advice. Boy, was that a journey. I'll talk more about this experience in the following chapters, but I learned and grew so much from this leadership role. I found my leadership style, I gained confidence, and Steve invested so much time and effort to mentor me. In *Be Obsessed or Be Average,* Grant Cardone writes that the biggest risk is doing nothing at all and the only way to reduce risk is to take risk. He uses the analogy that it is safer to be at sea than tied up to the harbor. Boats were made to be out on the water and decay when sitting on the dock.[51]

I wanted to quit so many times in my first leadership role but knew I had to push through and prove people wrong. I had to prove to others, and more importantly, myself, I could be successful at a young age. I made countless mistakes but continued to fail forward until I discovered the role wasn't the right fit for me, my future growth, and the trajectory of my career. Business with the airlines was drastically different than with private jets. I took a leadership position in an area that I did not know or understand, which was very risky! Many of my close mentors had warned me not to pursue it. I trusted my gut and pursued that growth opportunity. I found out it wasn't for me but did not regret my decision because I grew a lot from it and very quickly in the short time I was there.

I had set my sights on a project my original company was pursuing—a start-up location under construction in San Jose, California.

---
51 Grant Cardone, *Be Obsessed or Be Average* (Portfolio, October 11, 2016).

They were close to launching the location, so I decided to leave my leadership position and join the team. I was very familiar with the San Jose area because I went to school at San Jose State. The company had no experience in a startup so my manager at the time, Ken (he hired me on into the company into a front-line role) gave me the freedom to pave my own path and get things rolling. I wanted our team to be the best of the best in the company. I boldly set up training for the team and tailored the environment that best suited them. I took risks by launching various initiatives that were beyond the company standard, such as developing a paperless platform/process for internal processes, getting involved with the community, enhancing the overall customer experience, and extending appreciation to our customers in new ways. Our location quickly stole the spotlight, and company leadership and executives were beginning to notice us. Our performance was consistently stellar. There were a lot of unknowns but taking risks helped take our team to another level beyond what I had imagined.

In a Forbes article, Jason Hennessey mentions that "risks and taking action are necessary for success," and that understanding your risk appetite and tolerance enables you to take strategic actions.[52] The bolder I became and the more experience I acquired in taking risks, the greater my risk tolerance became. As a top performer within the company with the diverse experiences I had gained combined with my exposure to company executives, I was nominated to be a part of the launch of the company's leadership development program. It was a structured twelve-month program that would promote me into a senior leadership role. I was so

---

52 Jason Hennessey, "Striking a Balance Between Being Bold and Cautious in Business," *Forbes*, 3 Jul. 2023, https://www.forbes.com/sites/forbesagencycouncil/2023/07/03/striking-a-balance-between-being-bold-and-cautious-in-business/?sh=283fa30ad217.

eager to grow, and this was a great opportunity for me to achieve the next level of leadership. However, it would require relocating to New Jersey. I decided to accept the opportunity. It was my first time moving out of the house and living in my own place. I was so nervous about this opportunity, but it was a great experience, and under Pasquale's mentorship, I grew both personally and professionally beyond where I had been prior.

SMALL KEYS CAN OPEN UP BIG DOORS.

The lesson here is that it is okay to start small. One small, bold decision at a time can get you to big places. Small keys can open up big doors. And boy did the doors open up for me. It took some time, but they opened at the right time. So, start small. Go after that one small, bold decision. What's that small decision for you? You could be one small decision away from endless opportunities. About six months later, I got a phone call from my close long-term mentor Eric about some personnel changes in Southern California, and he asked if I had any interest. I took another leap of faith and said yes. After about six months in New Jersey, I once again picked up everything and moved to Southern California. Niall mentored me there. Both experiences—in New Jersey and California—were very different from each other, but I grew from both. After settling into this new location, I received another phone call from Eric. He sought to make my role as a middle manager permanent. I was hesitant but said yes because of the mentor-mentee relationship we had built over the years. After thinking about it for a few days, I realized that this role was not my goal and the purpose of being in the leadership development program was to achieve a senior leadership role. I called Eric back and said that I couldn't do it and that I had to stay focused on my ultimate goal of senior leadership. That conversation did not go well because I went against my word, and I felt really bad. I will never forget that conversation, but years later Eric and I reflected on this in Episode 1 of my podcast, he mentioned he was wrong to encourage me to stay at that location in a middle manager role.[53] I stayed true to my why which allowed me to be bold when I needed to be, even if it meant saying NO to an opportunity from my long-time mentor. I am so glad I remained bold and dared to say no because if I had followed through, the next opportunity to live in the Caribbean, where I experienced my greatest personal and professional growth, would not have come my way. Even if taking risks causes you to fall on your face and tick some people off, God will use that through promotion and reconciliation. You have to continue to push through.

THERE IS NEVER A RIGHT TIME TO TAKE A RISK. THE TIME IS NOW.

---

53 Eric Hietala, "Reflections of a Mentor-Mentee Relationship," *Navigation and Discovery with Cameron Singh*, podcast, episode 1, https://open.spotify.com/episode/2L96yUlmGHWVSEZgmBhqxq?si=f52505bd6d3f41a9.

In SUCCESS online magazine, Fauzia Burke mentions that "by being bold and pushing through fear . . . we actually grow and gain some control over the changes that happen to us."[54] Every change helps us realize our full potential. There is never a right time to take a risk. The time is now. What if I had not taken the risks that I did? Where would I be today? What if I had never tried and just played it safe?

I would encourage you to start taking risks. Be bold. It starts with little steps. The more risks you take, the greater your risk tolerance gets. If you fail, fail forward. If you succeed, you'll also move forward. Risk is being a part of something greater than ourselves to explore and grow our potential. Playing it safe puts the life you want at risk. Don't get so focused on the outcomes; they will take care of themselves and come forth as you take risks. Just take that first step. Open that door you thought was closed and walk through. I faced countless closed doors at a young age. I never was supposed to be in those leadership roles at my age. I had to open those doors on my own by faith. Trusting God through these risks and new opportunities strengthened my confidence in myself and God. I became convinced that God was by my side through it all. In the next chapter, we will turn our attention to boldness in faith and how it helped me throughout the journey of my early leadership years.

---

54 Fauzia Burke, "What I've Learned From Living Boldly and Taking Risks," *SUCCESS*, 26 Oct. 2016, https://www.success.com/what-ive-learned-from-living-boldly-and-taking-risks/#:~:text=I%20bet%20you%20are%20more,dreams%20down%20into%20small%20steps.

CHAPTER 6
BE BOLD IN FAITH

My faith as a Christian and believer in Jesus Christ is so important to me, especially being raised in the church through the influence of my mother. There were many times when I lost or neglected my faith to experience the worldly pleasures. I didn't always feel that God was not with me, but in retrospect, I see that He has been with me every step of the way in my life. Being in these new leadership positions at such a young age was not easy. I felt so unqualified and unprepared as the majority of the people I was leading were older and more experienced than me. It was only by the grace of God that I was able to gain the confidence and build my credibility to lead. There were people around me who told me I did not deserve to be in these leadership roles. Nevertheless, I continued to lean into my faith in God. If you want to become comfortable with taking risks, you first must learn to be bold in your faith. It was only through my faith in God that I was able to be bold and take the many risks that I took and continue to take. They didn't always work out the way I intended, but my boldness was rooted in my faith in God.

Growing up, I wasn't as open with my faith. I think it was because I didn't completely understand Christianity and didn't have a great understanding of the Bible. I kept my faith very close to me and slowly but surely, I started to open up a bit more about it around the end of my time in college. It was hard to be open because I wasn't the best example of a Christian, but I opened up when I simply started loving people just like Christ loves us. In John 15:12-13, the Bible says, "My command is this: Love each other as I have loved you. Greater love has no one than this: to lay down one's life for one's friends." That was exactly the posture I took to share my faith. That's what leadership is all about too—looking after and taking care of your people.

Before God developed my boldness, I had to surround myself with faith. I first developed a practice of going to church, diving into the Word, praying, listening to worship music and sermons in the car, and watching sermons on YouTube. This was my way of filling up my soul. Leadership involves a lot of responsibility in taking care of and looking after a team, both large or small. Remaining faithful in these practices equipped me to love people better. It was a way of filling my own cup so that I could lead well.

A lot of anxiety comes with taking risks, but my strong faith in God allowed me to lean on and trust Him. I gave it my all and let God do the rest. Sometimes it worked out, and sometimes it didn't work out, and that's completely okay. You can share the love of God with others through the work you do. I learned this through attending the Hillsong Conference in 2016 and the Catalyst Leadership Conference. I learned that your faith can be a part of everything you do.

Psalm 37:23 says, "The LORD makes firm the steps of the one who delights in him." This verse means that the Lord directs the steps of the godly and delights in every detail of their lives. It also means that everything will work out for good for those who love God and follow His will. It's easy to read but difficult to apply. Stepping out in faith to pursue something big can be very difficult because it means journeying into the unknown. As I mentioned in the last chapter, opening a door is not easy to do, but faith is what helped me open up those doors. In *The Most Valuable Catch*, Steve Jamison writes, "Sometimes, God is very patient in giving us plenty of clues that he wants us to trust Him for more, but at other times the choice must be made quickly."[55] There were many times when I had to make decisions very quickly both in new leadership roles or in transition to the next phase of my leadership journey.

GOD'S PURPOSE FOR HIS CHILDREN IS THAT THEY WIN AND CONTINUE TO WIN.

I became bold in leadership only after I learned to trust God and know that He was always with me. Of course, I felt discouraged if something didn't work out, but my faith and trust in God enabled me to move forward and try the next thing. 1 Corinthians 9:24 says, "Do you not know that in a race all the runners run,

---

[55] Steve Jamison, *The Most Valuable Catch: Risking It All for What Matters the Most* (Sanford, FL: AVAIL, July 25, 2023).

but only one gets the prize? Run in such a way as to get the prize." In this verse, Paul compares living in service to Christ to an athletic competition. He encourages the Corinthians to join him in running the race of life to win. God's purpose for His children is that they win and continue to win. God will take us through some things to help prepare us for the next thing. When things didn't work out in my favor, I determined that God was preparing me for something else.

In *You Can Live the Dream*, Nick Nilson says, "Your step of faith can give the permission to step as well."[56] I didn't realize this as a new leader. My steps of faith and boldness in taking risks allowed others around me to do the same. I experienced this when I promoted others around me, coached the people I led, and helped them believe that they were made for more.

For some of you, faith may not be a part of your life, and you may believe in something else when it comes to spirituality and religion. This chapter intends to show how faith emboldened me to take those leaps of faith and jump into the next big uncomfortable thing or the next leadership role. If you would like to learn more about my faith journey, tune in to my faith podcast, *Divine Revelations Unleashed*. More info can be found in the Appendix.

Take some time to reflect on what needs to happen in order for you to take that next opportunity. Are you missing something? Do you feel an emptiness? I encourage you to learn more about faith and spirituality and how they can help you in your leadership journey.

---

[56] Nilson, *You Can Live the Dream*.

CHAPTER 7

GET OUT OF YOUR COMFORT ZONE AND SET YOURSELF APART

Getting out of my comfort zone and setting myself apart played a huge role in my success in the workforce and still does today. Why is this important for you? Why is it even important to think about getting out of your comfort zone?

I could not settle for mediocrity. In one of Pastor Steven Furtick's sermons, he mentions that living in comfort can keep you from your calling.[57] The power of God will be silenced in your life when you live in comfort and play it safe. Life will pass you by if you choose to live in your comfort zone.

Getting out of my comfort zone was a huge challenge for me and it started when I was preparing for college in my high school years. I am a first-generation college student and wanted to pursue an aviation career, which was very nontraditional compared to my peers. I also stepped out of my comfort zone when I pursued

---
[57] Steven Furtick, "The Danger of Comfort," Filmed July 19, 2019 at Elevation Church, *YouTube*, https://www.youtube.com/watch?v=VZXyCwokQh8.

community college courses in high school. I attended my high school classes during the day and my college classes in the evening. I even took online classes, at times stacking twelve to eighteen units in a semester because I wanted to get ahead of the game. I wanted to set myself apart and be my own person. I did not want to be like others and take the traditional route. I loved taking community college classes as I got to meet new people. I loved every part of it. While my classmates in high school struggled through IB and advanced courses (which I never enjoyed), I took these courses at the local community college and got ahead. By the time I graduated high school, I had achieved an Associate of Arts degree.

LIFE WILL PASS YOU BY IF YOU CHOOSE TO LIVE IN YOUR COMFORT ZONE.

Simon Sinek shares how he actually *finds* his comfort in making himself uncomfortable by challenging his thinking and exposing himself to different experiences.[58] The process of seeking, engaging, and feeling these experiences is the foundation of his approach, regardless of the result. It has informed his thinking on leadership. He believes that embracing discomfort and the uncomfortable—in short, curiosity—is an essential

---

58 Simon Sinek, "Simon Sinek in Finding Comfort in the Uncomfortable and Unfamiliar," Filmed Jan. 30, 2022, *YouTube*, https://www.youtube.com/watch?v=fpnlSc4pH7I.

leadership skill. I maintained that curiosity through my college years and in my first job in the aviation industry.

My first job in the industry came from my involvement in an industry networking group called the Northern California Business Aviation Association in college. I was such a timid and reserved person during this time and the idea of networking was terrifying, but I knew it was something I needed to do to learn more about the aviation industry. I had to step out of my comfort zone and I gained the confidence to interact with other aviation professionals without realizing I would meet my first employer at one of the networking events. None of my classmates attended these networking events. I was one of the few students who attended, and I stood out because I was consistent. I eventually became a board member for the organization after volunteering for a few years.

During my time in front-line roles in the aviation industry, I made sure to execute my job to the fullest and the best that I could. I had my eyes set on leadership growth, but to set myself apart from the team, I first had to get to know them. Once I got to know each person on my team on an individual level, they supported my aspirations. They gained an understanding of my trajectory, and it helped set me apart from the team. I gave feedback to my managers on where we could improve in the work environment. Additionally, I remained curious about the business because I was hungry to learn. I always asked my peers, leaders, executives, and the corporate staff questions. I worked a lot of overtime during staffing challenges when no one else would. My curiosity motivated me to step up to the plate and help where I was needed. I loved what I did, and I wanted to learn more about the business. As I added more value to the work environment, I started to set myself apart. I was not just another team member but someone the leaders could rely on for special operations or when they needed help.

Where is your comfort zone, and what do you need to do to break free of living in it and get uncomfortable? And this is how you grow.

> ## YOU WERE CREATED TO LIVE OUTSIDE OF YOUR COMFORT ZONE AND ARE CALLED FOR HIGHER.

It's not easy to break out of your comfort zone but the more you do it, the easier it gets. The first step is to become comfortable with being uncomfortable. Deuteronomy 14:2 says, "You have been set apart as holy to the LORD your God, and he has chosen you from all the nations of the earth to be his special treasure." God created you as His special treasure. You were created to live outside of your comfort zone and are called for higher. It starts with believing that you are made to soar higher.

As Dr. Sam Chand says, "The only person standing between you and your next level is you."[59] It's natural for us to find security in our comfort zone, but if you stay there, you will not go any higher than where you are now.

---

[59] Dr. Sam Chand, "The Need for Constant Improvement," *Sam Chand Blog*, https://www.samchand.com/blog/the-need-for-constant-improvement.

In my early leadership roles, I always felt the need for constant improvement. Dr. Chand states,
> It doesn't matter how good you are. You have to improve constantly. How? Start by not believing what they say. The moment you start believing their praises and admiration—thinking you're all that and a bag of chips—you'll stop improving.[60]

MY FOCUS WAS TO GET BETTER AND BETTER, AND GETTING BETTER WAS ONLY GOING TO HAPPEN THROUGH CRITICISM.

I always looked for ways to take things to the next level in everything I did, whether in leadership or something for the team. This was a process. When I first started in the workforce, I had a lot of ideas on how to make things better in my front-line roles, but I often hesitated to offer that feedback. I started with small pieces of periodic feedback and became more comfortable and less fearful of what my manager would think of me. I did not want to come off as too arrogant or a "snobby college grad." To my earlier point, criticism was very difficult to receive because I thought I was doing something wrong, or people were trying to put me down. In retrospect, I realize that people were just trying to help me. Once I saw myself growing and learning, I started to

---
60 Chand, *Blog*.

take feedback more seriously. I didn't think much of the praises; instead, my focus was to get better and better, and getting better would only happen through criticism. In fact, I asked my managers for criticism and feedback every opportunity I got.

John Maxwell calls it "stretching with intention."[61] The constant search for improvement was a huge driver throughout my leadership journey. The search never felt obligatory because hunger for growth has been part of my DNA since high school. I never wanted a break from finding ways to set myself apart.

As I mentioned in an earlier chapter, your why will make a debut in the process of setting yourself apart. During my time in Southern California, we had a newly promoted leadership team. I observed each of them struggle in different areas; they were in dire need of coaching and leadership development. So, I established leadership development plans with each of them and met with them once a week to focus on their development. This was not something that the company required, but it was something I wanted to do to take our team to the next level.

IT TAKES SMALL STEPS OF ACTION TO GET COMFORTABLE IN THE UNCOMFORTABLE.

---

61 John Maxwell, "Leadership—When It Matters Most: Stretch Statements," Filmed 10 June 2020, *YouTube*, https://www.youtube.com/watch?v=Zw6GcMpnIU0.

Get Out of Your Comfort Zone and Set Yourself Apart 97

I was already out of my comfort zone in planning for the launch of our San Jose location. I continued to focus on the team and customers as early as opening day. As a leadership team, we worked together and sought feedback from team members and customers to take our company to new heights. You'll face negative feedback but remember that it is for the team's greater good. To get out of your comfort zone as a leader, especially as a new leader, is to have difficult conversations, be vulnerable, and address failure.

I continued to stay true to my why and, over time, that is what set me apart. It takes small steps of action to get comfortable in the uncomfortable. Joanna Howes' model on comfort illustrates why leaders must escape their comfort zones.

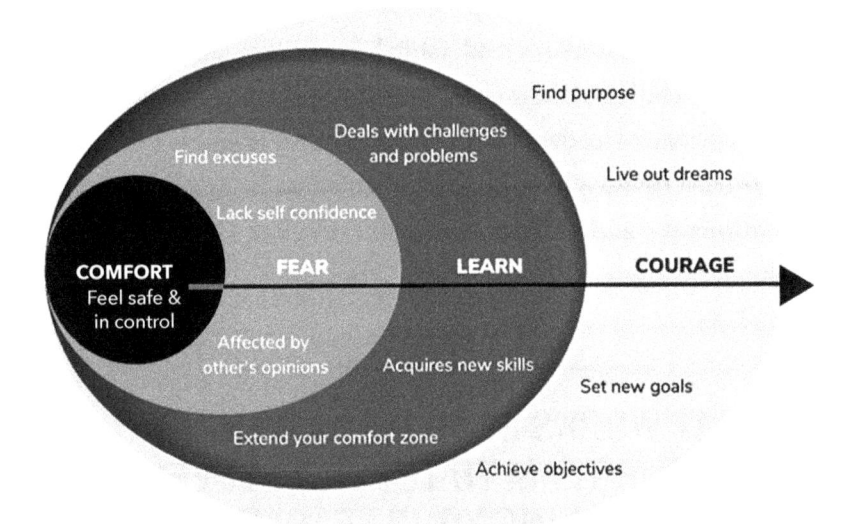

COMFORT — Feel safe & in control

FEAR — Find excuses, Lack self confidence, Affected by other's opinions, Extend your comfort zone

LEARN — Deals with challenges and problems, Acquires new skills

COURAGE — Find purpose, Live out dreams, Set new goals, Achieve objectives

Howes asserts that curiosity for learning is the key to conquering our fears because it produces courage to step out into discomfort. Joanna mentions that we must be ready to trust the process and learn from those who have gone before us to achieve the success we want to reach and access our full potential.[62]

Learn how to navigate through constant and continuous improvement. Seeking leadership development through attending conferences, reading books, listening to podcasts, and the like helped me become a new and effective leader. Your efforts to learn and develop will extend out in the work that you do and eventually, you will notice that you have set yourself apart. When you set yourself apart, you also set yourself up for further growth. You have something special to offer, so stay true to your why and don't lose sight of it so that you can inspire others around you. First, lead by example, and then find ways to add value to your organization with high integrity. Many leaders I worked with did not set a good example of leadership because they were dishonest, ultimately leading to their termination. I could never compromise my integrity as a leader because I could never imagine losing my team's trust in me. I have done everything so far as a leader with intentionality, and I follow through. I do what I say, which is a highly important trait to carry in leadership.

IT WORKS BOTH WAYS: TAKING YOUR TEAM TO THE NEXT LEVEL AND TAKING YOUR LEADERSHIP TO THE NEXT LEVEL.

---

[62] Joanna Howes, "Why leaders need to move out of their comfort zone" LinkedIn post, *LinkedIn*, 25 May 2021, https://www.linkedin.com/pulse/why-leaders-need-move-out-comfort-zone-joanna-howes/.

Inspiring your team and empowering your team allows you to set yourself apart. It was rewarding to see leaders witness their growth from the creative leadership development plans we created together. The team saw their leadership improve, and that set me apart because I had put in the time and effort to get them there. As a result, my boss received great feedback from the team about me over time and they saw the newly promoted leaders developing and growing.

Leading through your actions with great intentionality goes a long way. It works both ways: taking your team to the next level and taking your leadership to the next level.

You may not have the experience to do this but start small. Take small steps to get out of your comfort zone. Stretch yourself with intentionality and look for ways to elevate yourself and your team. Above all, take ownership when you fail. Your team wins when you own your mistakes because it shows them that you are imperfect and learning, as well. I made a big scheduling error one time with my team around the holidays; I accidentally approved too many time off requests over the holidays. Once I learned of my mistake, I was there to support the team, apologized to them publicly, and took responsibility for the error on my part the very next day. The feedback was great. After all, the team respected me a bit more because I admitted I was in the wrong. It is a difficult thing to do, but it will earn you the trust and respect of your team that you need.

Do start with yourself to set yourself apart—that is not true leadership. True leadership is looking after your team, inspiring them, and taking them and the organization to the next level. That's how you set yourself apart and set yourself up to be a successful leader.

CHAPTER 8
PURSUE GROWTH IN FAITH

The word GROWTH has a lot of meaning. Growth has been a huge part of my life, and I had to be very intentional about it to move forward personally and professionally and as a man of faith. John Maxwell encourages people to "pursue a lifetime of growth not just because it will make them better, or open new doors" but because "growth increases hope."[63] Over time, growth creates a momentum that then begets more growth. Planting the seed of growth is not complicated. It's as simple as a change in mindset. When we decide to believe that growth is possible and commit to pursuing it, hope rises. The change in focus is only the first step, but it can be the beginning of a long and rewarding journey. When I am not growing or spending time in growth pursuits, I realize that my day-to-day becomes stale and mediocrity settles in my leadership.

---
[63] John C. Maxwell, "The Most Important Reason to Pursue Growth," *John C. Maxwell Blog*, https://www.johnmaxwell.com/blog/the-most-important-reason-to-pursue-growth/#:~:text=When%20you%20make%20growth%20a,of%20difference%20to%20you%20today.

My interest in growth started back in grade school. I always wanted to learn more beyond what was taught. I used to go above and beyond in my schoolwork because I had already developed that posture of learning. This also was rooted from my mother always encouraging me to go above and beyond as this is what she practices in her daily work and personal life. I have learned that growth starts with taking those small steps every single day. Those small steps will breed consistent growth.

For example, if you wake up at 6 a.m., it may make a difference to wake up at 5 a.m. instead—a small shift that can change the trajectory of your day. Robin Sharma wrote a really good book on the benefits of waking up at 5 a.m. and how it can transform your life. I normally spend the first few hours of my day writing, podcast editing, planning out the day, and "me" time. During this time, I don't have many phone calls or emails come through, so it is the quietest time of my day. Robin Sharma has a 20-20-20 method: Wake up at 5 a.m., spend twenty minutes exercising, twenty minutes in prayer or reflection, and twenty minutes focused on personal growth.[64] I'm not saying that you need to wake up at 5am. Do what works best for you and the way you are wired. This is only a starting point, but you can make those first few hours of the day your own and do what works best for you. Maybe it's a great time for you to respond to emails, go to the gym, or pray and do your devotional. I sometimes play a sermon on YouTube in the morning during breakfast or if I am working on something that doesn't require a lot of focus. Growth starts small.

---

64 Robin Sharma, *The 5 AM Club: Own Your Morning. Elevate Your Life* (New York, NY: HarperCollins, January 7, 2020).

James Clear validates the power of creating small, daily habits in his book *Atomic Habits*.[65] To grow, you must stretch yourself where you are. Set goals for areas where you want to grow personally, professionally, and in your faith if that's something part of you. For me, growth started with curiosity. I wanted to learn more about leadership, I wanted to learn more about the Christian faith, and I wanted to learn more about the aviation industry. My curiosity started when I first attended the 2016 Hillsong Conference where I learned more about influence, leadership, and faith. I purchased many of the books and resources available from the speakers such as Craig Groeschel, Erwin McManus, Steven Furtick, Brian Houston, and Christine Caine. I read their books, watched their YouTube sermons, and listened to podcasts. I broadened my horizons on my faith, leadership, and influence.

I purchased and read more books from other pastors, business leaders, and motivational speakers. I became particularly interested in leadership and wanted to learn more about it as I was in a new leadership role in the aviation industry. I knew very little about leadership and was still finding my way in the new role. I knew I wanted to pursue a doctorate, so I ended up pursuing a doctorate in executive leadership at the University of Charleston. My leadership grew so much from this experience as the program was not only focused on teaching leadership theories, but it was also focused on application and what you can add to the body of knowledge of executive leadership. My pursuit of my doctorate started with curiosity.

What are you curious about? Do you feel like you are destined for more? My growth journey started with these questions. According

---

65 James Clear, *Atomic Habits: An Easy & Proven Way to Build Good Habits & Break Bad Ones* (Avery, October 16, 2018).

to Transcend Health, "personal growth is the process of an individual becoming aware of the 'self' in its entirety, followed by taking steps to address the behavior, attitudes, values, actions, and habits that they wish to change."[66] As I mentioned earlier, personal growth for me started in grade school. In middle school, I also developed interests in politics, photography, film, and creative writing. I volunteered in the church media department that I grew up in. I watched the news, particularly ABC World News Tonight, and learned about politics. I loved writing but was terrible at math and science. There was no hope for me in those subjects! I failed calculus twice in college, barely passed the third time, and also failed accounting. I knew aviation was going to be my "career path," and the rest of my interests became hobbies. I used our home video camera and recorded random moments on trips for fun. My parents bought me video editing software so that I could produce video summaries of all our trips. I taught myself video editing from online videos. I learned even more about film and photography through my involvement in church as part of productions.

> **IF YOU WANT TO CHANGE THE WORLD AND MAKE IT A BETTER PLACE FOR ALL, YOU NEED TO START WITH ITS LEADERS.**

---

[66] "Why Is Personal Growth Important?" *Transcend Health*, https://www.transcendhealth.com.au/why-is-personal-growth-important/.

My Hillsong Conference experience set me on a journey of curiosity and longing for more. I continued to learn from leadership resources, including several leadership events and conferences such as Catalyst and The Global Leadership Summit. I paid my way in travel, hotel, and conference fees and then spent even more on the resources and books they sold. I liked that I was learning not only from pastors but also from business leaders of all types, along with political and educational leaders. I saw the value of attending these conferences in Atlanta, Los Angeles, Chicago, and across the United States. One time I even drove five hours to Hershey, Pennsylvania while living in New Jersey to see Craig Groeschel and Brian Houston for a one-day Catalyst leadership event. My mentor Pasquale was gracious enough to give me the day off for that. I was so hungry to grow and broaden my understanding of leadership and that hunger remains today. I want to continue to stretch myself and take my personal growth to the next level.

Psychology Today says that one "key ingredient to personal growth is finding a teacher or teachers that we can learn from on our journey. The reason this is a key ingredient is that it's helpful to have an expert in the subject who can help us understand these principles more deeply."[67] In *Pilot*, author Nicholas John mentions that leaders have a singular effect on shaping our world—both past and present.[68] This is how it has been, and this is how it will always be. So, if you want to change the world and make it a better place for all, you need to start with its leaders. Curiosity lends itself to both personal growth and career growth. I remember when I first started in the aviation industry and fell in love with

---
67 Robert Puff, "The Path to Personal Growth," *Psychology Today*, 13 June 2021, https://www.psychologytoday.com/us/blog/meditation-modern-life/202106/the-path-personal-growth.
68 Nicholas John, *Pilot: Preparing Integral Leaders of Tomorrow* (Inspire, September 28, 2021).

the company I was working for at the time, I applied for senior leadership roles regularly while in front-line roles. I wanted to grow quickly and achieve my goal of being a senior leader. I didn't realize that it would be a process that would require patience and patience is a trait I am still trying to work on. I had to trust the process. Traveling to other locations and learning more about the business and company helped significantly. I paid to attend industry-wide conferences because I wanted to interact with the company executives and other corporate staff. As I mentioned earlier, this is how I gained my first leadership role with the sister company. Even though this was a short-lived role, I learned so much about my leadership style and how to truly lead people. Even though I may not have been the best leader, I grew so much from that experience.

When I transitioned to the San Jose location, my leadership expanded in that role and I continued to stand out to my team. I was one of two team members selected to be a part of the company's leadership development program launch. I relocated to New Jersey for six months and then to Southern California for another six months. At the end of this program, I was given the opportunity to take a role abroad in the Caribbean. I took that opportunity even though it was risky. I am so glad I did not play it safe and pursue other opportunities that were open at the time in Roanoke, Virginia, or Midland, Texas. Living abroad in the Caribbean in Antigua and Barbuda was such a refreshing opportunity as a senior leader.

TO GROW IN YOUR CAREER, YOU HAVE TO GIVE IT ALL YOU'VE GOT WHERE YOU CURRENTLY ARE.

I was probably too aggressive with my career growth, especially with the first aviation company I worked for, but as I look back, I see how much I grew in such a short period. I was also given opportunities to live in places I would have never lived on my own. Pursuing growth afforded me unique opportunities that very few were offered. I never took advantage of these opportunities because of the level of work I put into opening these doors. I continued to give it my all, stand out, and make a name for myself. To grow in your career, you have to give it all you've got where you currently are. I was permitted to travel, seek new opportunities, and live in different parts of the world because I continued to perform well in my current role. Never lose sight of where you are and allow promotion and success to get to your head.

Voicing where I wanted to go in my career helped me early on and this is something I learned from my mentor, Eric. I made it known to my peers, managers, and company executives that my ultimate goal was to be in a senior leadership role. I garnered so much support simply because I voiced what I wanted. My managers provided me with opportunities to accomplish that goal.

VISION IS NOT PERMANENT; IT'S PROGRESSIVE.

Another thing that helped me was openness to shifting in another direction. I never thought that I would leave the company I was with after being with them for almost a decade. In his book *Take Your Seat,* Dr. Jermone Glenn mentions that it's okay to re-vision your vision while in pursuit of purpose. He says, "Vision is not permanent; it's progressive."[69] I realized that I had grown the highest I could with the company I was in, and that further growth would be slow if I stayed. I transitioned to other opportunities after that and re-visioned the trajectory of my career. I initially thought that I would be with my first company for longer and become a company executive. However, my goal shifted to entrepreneurship. I gained other interests, such as real estate, and I have a company now that focuses on short-term rentals and other real estate investments. I am working on other new ventures because I want to work for myself and have the freedom to enjoy life, travel, and build streams of passive income for myself. This path, such as writing this book, makes room for greater impact by helping others strive for higher.

Growing in faith was a huge part of my pursuit of personal growth and career growth. My curiosity and drive for further understanding of Christianity grew after the Hillsong Conference. I began to read faith books and learn more about the Bible. I started to watch sermons from other churches online such as Elevation Church, Hillsong Church, Vous Church, Zoe Church, Life Church,

---

[69] Dr. Jermone Glenn, *Take Your Seat: Discover Your Significance* (Sanford, FL: AVAIL, August 29, 2023), 39.

Free Chapel and Mosaic. I learned so much from these pastors, and I got involved in the local church. I had a great community surrounding me. To pursue growth in faith, I had to remove many of the worldly pleasures that were not adding value to my life.

In *Stand Up*, author René Banglesdorf mentions "if you want to be successful in the things that matter most, you must learn to say no to things that don't align with the legacy you are building. You may not have to cut things out completely but learn how to limit them."[70] It was difficult to consistently grow in my faith. Personal and career growth often interfered with the growth of my faith. It was difficult to keep faith a priority. I needed God so much during those times of uncertainty, fear, and anxiety about the next new thing, but He gave me so many rich experiences and allowed me to live in some pretty cool places that helped my career growth. God brought all those opportunities my way for a purpose. *Confronting Compromise*, author Joe Champion mentions that "the day you stop growing, you stop living as God desires."[71]

I never found an effective rhythm in my life for consistent devotion time and still struggle with that today. I sporadically turned on YouTube sermons when I felt my soul needed it. I would read and go through plans on the Bible App. I would occasionally open the Word and go through books of the Bible using Zach Windahl's Bible Study Guide. I would occasionally journal when I felt things were difficult and needed to write out my prayers to God.

Ultimately, I did not have a consistent rhythm that helped me grow in my faith. I pursued growth through various avenues

---
70 René Banglesdorf, *Stand Up: How to Flourish When the Odds Are Stacked Against You* (New York, NY: Morgan James Publishing, April 9, 2019), 38-39.
71 Joe Champion, Twitter post, Oct. 19, 2022, 10:47 am, https://x.com/joechampion/status/1582745159766114305.

which helped stretch my faith. It was the small habits, such as listening to worship music while working, listening to faith podcasts on a long drive, or watching a sermon on YouTube. Chip Ingram and Francis Chan encourage us to find some time with the Lord and not let anything replace that.[72] Despite the difficulty, the more I make the time to grow in my faith, the more I see growth both personally and professionally. Even today, I don't have a great rhythm in pursuing growth in my faith, but I still find time to read the Bible and watch sermons. I also regularly attend faith-based conferences with some of the churches that I follow online. When an opportunity comes up for a conference or event, I attend, no matter where it is. For me, the ways I grow in my faith have no limits, and it all started with saving up and traveling to Sydney, Australia for the Hillsong Conference in 2016 where I rededicated my life to Christ.

Take some time to reflect. What shifts do you need to make to be intentional in your personal and professional growth? What drives your curiosity? Discover what makes you tick, even if it is irrelevant to your professional life. We are all imperfect people, so learning should never end. In her book *Living with Purpose*, Michelle Hubert mentions that the gift of imperfection is that it teaches us the necessity of learning to extend and receive grace.[73] So get curious and seek growth in faith!

In the next chapter, we will discuss how to lead responsibly in faith. Throughout my journey so far, I have seen leaders fall short because of irresponsible leadership. Responsible leadership is difficult but the rewards are greater.

---

72 Chip Ingram and Francis Chan, "Pursuing Personal Growth," Filmed 28 Oct. 2015 at Living on the Edge, *YouTube*, https://www.youtube.com/watch?v=FlmUUGwtmDY.
73 Hubert, *Living with Purpose*, 144.

CHAPTER 9

LEAD RESPONSIBLY IN FAITH

With leadership comes great responsibility. Leadership is a lot to take in for new and seasoned leaders alike. Multiple aspects of leadership are overwhelming—learning your job, getting to know your team, and understanding what is expected of you. This is also known as the Peter Parker principle from Spiderman—with great power comes great responsibility. You can't take your leadership role lightly. That's irresponsible leadership. Instead, take leadership seriously, set the example, and be in it with your team. Being a leader is both a burden and rewarding. In his book *The Life-Giving Leader*, Tyler Reagin discusses how life-giving leadership does not happen when you're sitting on the sideline, at either work or on the field. "Hard work and sweat are often the hallmarks of great leaders." Leaders need not to be afraid to get dirty, work long hours, and they need to dig in and be in it with their teams.[74]

---

[74] Tyler Reagin, *The Life-Giving Leader: Learning to Lead from Your Truest Self* (Colorado Springs, CO: WaterBrook, September 18, 2018), 111.

I have observed irresponsible leaders throughout my journey in the workforce who fell short in integrity and tried to cut corners; they were selfish and always put themselves first before their team. Don't get me wrong, it is important to look after yourself as a leader, but you are there to lead your team and be there for them. I observed leaders who were determined to make themselves look good and take credit for other people's work and wins to make themselves look good. I have seen that these types of leaders do not last. I have seen leaders' lack of integrity catch up to them, and they get caught cutting corners or taking advantage of a company credit card. Based on my experience with these types of leaders, I made it of utmost importance to lead responsibly. Leading with integrity was a huge focus for me because I did not want my team to lose their trust in me. I wanted to build credibility with my team, especially as a young leader. I did not have the courage or urge to cut corners even though the opportunities to do so were there and the temptation was even greater. In his book *Leveling Up*, Ryan Leak states that as leaders, each and every one of us has a moment in our lives where we have the opportunity to do the right thing but are tempted to do the wrong thing, especially if we can get away with it.[75]

When you lie, you lose trust. Lying results in a loss of trust, which is challenging to regain and effortless to diminish. Losing trust can have severe consequences, such as losing a job or damaging relationships with family and friends. To progress in both personal and professional aspects, it is crucial to prioritize building trust with the individuals we interact with regularly.

---

[75] Ryan Leak, *Leveling Up: 12 Questions to Elevate Your Personal and Professional Development* (Nashville, TN: Thomas Nelson, December 6, 2022).

This requires maintaining a high level of integrity, as acting with a lack of integrity not only damages our connections with others but also affects our relationship with ourselves and degrades our leadership. When our team starts to lose their trust in you as a leader this can be a true showstopper for you in leadership as recovering from distrust is a difficult journey.

YOUR TEAM CAN COUNT ON YOU AND TRUST YOU TO THE EXTENT THAT YOU ARE WHO YOU SAY YOU ARE.

Integrity means authenticity, openness, and transparency. I knew that was the only way I could gain trust as a young leader and now as a seasoned leader. Many did not trust me initially because of my young age and lack of experience. It was only through being open, transparent, and authentic that I started to gain credibility. When I didn't know how to do something, I admitted it and leaned on the team for help. I saw other leaders come with the attitude and posture that they knew everything when they really didn't, and it showed in their work performance and how they led the team or organization. I lost great trust in those leaders. The posture of a "what you see is what you get" mindset went a long way for me in gaining credibility from my team. Your team can count on you and trust you to the extent that you are who you say you are. Who you are in public often matches who you are in private. Who you are when no one is watching is a great part of leading with high integrity when it aligns with who you are in the spotlight. You will lose integrity when you try to bend the rules to get something you really, really want. I have seen this happen, especially when leaders want to grow quickly. They try to cut corners and bend the rules, but that never works out for them. As Ryan Leak says, "Choose integrity. It may cost you more time and energy in the process, but when you succeed, you'll know you did it with honor."[76]

Transparency is also essential to leading responsibly because it nurtures accountability. Your leadership team and other team members have permission to hold you accountable. I enjoyed it when others were honest with me about something they disagreed with because it showed they were comfortable in holding me accountable. At first, it can be very uncomfortable, but as leaders that's where we need to be—comfortable in the uncomfortable. Responsible leadership goes out the door when a leader gets too comfortable. For example, poor decisions, subpar execution in workplace changes, or providing insufficient resources for your team all stem from comfortability. I made so many mistakes over the years as a leader, but when I was transparent with the team about it, they accepted my mistakes because I showed them who I was—a person of high character. When a leader consistently takes responsibility for their actions, it shows they'll be dependable when things get tough and that they embrace accountability for their actions and behavior. These leaders "lead by example, can be counted on in all types of situations and scenarios, and are not afraid to make difficult decisions."[77] It's not easy to admit

---
76 Leak, *Leveling Up*, 127.
77 Mara Calvello, "7 Ways to Take Responsibility as a Leader," *Fellow*, 6 Apr. 2022, https://fellow.app/blog/management/ways-to-take-responsibility-as-a-leader/.

your mistakes, both big and small, but it is so worth it. I have led teams across the United States and abroad, and I can tell you that admission and ownership go a long way. In *Turbo Leadership*, Dr. Sam Chand says that "when you're honest with your people, your authenticity, genuineness, and integrity will rise to a higher level with them, and they will know you are a truth-teller."[78] This is huge when it comes to leading responsibly.

Getting in the trenches with your team is also an important part of leading responsibly, and sometimes this involves getting a bit dirty. Leadership is not all about suits and ties and nicely polished shoes. I first learned this from my first leader, Kenny that I worked with. Kenny's leadership style came from his experience as an officer in the Navy. He dressed sharply every day and interacted with his team at the start of every day. He never started his day going to his office. He first made the effort to engage with the team. Whenever we got busy, he was unafraid to roll up his sleeves, get dirty, and help wherever he could. He stayed long hours during times we were short-staffed. I came to respect him tremendously and still have great respect for him to this day because that quality about him has never changed. He was always in it with his team, and I knew I would strive to do the same whenever I rose to a leadership position. As a leader, you have to be the one they can lean on, especially in difficult times.

I walked into complete chaos when I stepped into my first leadership role and oversaw around 200 team members. If I wanted to be "in it" with my team, I had to work long hours during the first few months until things stabilized. Tyler Reagin encourages

---

[78] Sam Chand, *Turbo Leadership: Power Points for Maximum Performance* (Sanford, FL: AVAIL, May 30, 2023), 37.

us not to fear getting dirty.[79] In my leadership role at San Jose, I put in the hours to support the team so that they knew they could rely on me as a leader. I continue to practice this because I have never forgotten what I witnessed in Kenny.

Despite the sacrifices you must make to become a responsible leader, you also need to take care of yourself. I believe self-care is the most important part of responsible leadership. I faced burnout very quickly in my first leadership role because I was *too* in it with the team. I was so in it that I lost sight of myself. I was too invested in being there for my team. It's important to find that balance between work and other responsibilities, like family and taking care of yourself. I only lived a few minutes away from work in my first leadership role, and I would come home literally only to sleep, so I burned out quickly. In San Jose, I started early and stayed late because I was so invested and proud of what we built at that location, not only our team but a stellar operation. Eventually, that was no longer sustainable, and I faced burnout again. In *Leadership Unleashed*, Todd Bishop admonishes that "leaders must take a break or they will break".[80] And yes, I did break. I was adapting to these new leadership roles and pursuing graduate school at the same time, so I was busy. If I wasn't working, I was studying. It was a big wake-up call for me and I had to recalibrate myself and find a better balance.

I had the opportunity to interview Christy Wright on an episode of my podcast. We discussed her book *Take Back Your Time*, and she talked about how we have to redefine balance and what it means for us individually. She mentioned that life balance isn't

---

[79] Reagin, *The Life-Giving Leader*.
[80] Todd R. Bishop, *Leadership Unleashed: Take Your Life to Another Level* (Sanford, FL: AVAIL, February 1, 2023), 221.

about doing everything for an equal amount of time. Life balance is about doing the right things at the right time. It's about spending your one life on what matters to you. Traditionally, when we think of balance, we think of work-life balance and the focus should not be on that, it should be you finding the balance that works for you.[81] It has been a really difficult journey to figure out what balance was and is for me. I struggle with it even today. One thing that I discovered in my conversation with Christy was that it is difficult to find the balance in your life because different seasons will require new priority shifts and diverting your attention to what matters the most in that season. I had to put the work into stabilizing the team and operation but did not create proper boundaries for myself. In San Jose, I had to devote more hours and time to ensure a great launch for the site but had poor boundaries. The lessons I learned helped me in writing my first book. I carved out time to write and set boundaries so that I could still travel, play golf with friends, and read. After burning out a few times, I learned that the only way to find balance is to set boundaries.

> **AFTER BURNING OUT A FEW TIMES, I LEARNED THAT THE ONLY WAY TO FIND BALANCE IS TO SET BOUNDARIES.**

---

81 Christy Wright, "Take Back Your Time," *Navigation and Discovery with Cameron Singh*, podcast, episode 4, https://open.spotify.com/episode/6EcLDZ2epf4vVIn7SmgIKw?si=a3d71ffd080841ec.

In his book *Balance*, Touré Roberts writes that the person who will find balance must learn the discipline of regularly muting life's noise. We must learn to conserve our yes for the things that matter most, and the only way to do that is to have a hefty amount of no's in our lives.[82] This is exactly why I burnt out because I was saying yes to everything and became overloaded with work along with my other tasks and responsibilities.

One thing that I learned over the years was that the more I found balance, the better leader I was. I slept better, was better prepared, and was more present and active in the work environment. In *At Your Best*, Carey Nieuwhof advises instead of managing your time, focus on managing your energy.[83] He categorizes energy levels as green (times when you are most alert and creative), yellow (times when you have moderate energy levels), and red (times when you don't have much energy and can't be very productive). I learned that I am most creative during the early morning hours and after dinner time. So, I tend to do my writing and creative endeavors during those hours that involve deeper thinking. I have been able to rearrange my day to complete tasks when my energy levels are optimal rather than when they are at their lowest.

Take some time to reflect on where you are with balance and what shifts you need to make to find a balance that works for you in the season that you are in.

A lot of weight and responsibility comes with leadership and as new leaders, it's tempting to feel "you have arrived," but know that

---

[82] Touré Roberts, *Balance: Positioning Yourself to Do Things Well* (Grand Rapids, MI: Zondervan, April 26, 2022).
[83] Carey Nieuwhof, *At Your Best: How to Get Time, Energy, and Priorities Working in Your Favor* (Colorado Springs, CO: WaterBrook, September 14, 2021).

it is only the beginning of your leadership journey. It gets harder and harder, but it is so rewarding when you allow the weight and burden of leadership to shape you into a responsible leader. Be a leader of high integrity, find that balance for yourself, and be in it with your team, and you will go far in leadership. As Dr. Sam Chand mentions in his book *Turbo Leadership*, "Leadership is not a role. It is not something you do. It's a responsibility related to who you are."[84]

---

84 Chand, *Turbo Leadership*.

CHAPTER 10
REMAIN HUMBLE IN FAITH

Humility can transform your leadership journey, but building it into your leadership doesn't come without difficulties. When I was promoted as a new leader for the first time at the age of twenty-one, I was so prideful at first, but I learned quickly that it was not all about me; it was all about the team and people whom I was leading. I remember my parents telling me as I started going to school and working to never forget where I came from, and I took that to heart. So many people were cheering me on and helped me earn my first promotion. I couldn't have been promoted on my own.

Management Consulted mentions that "leaders come in all shapes and sizes. Some are extroverts who are natural-born motivators, while others are introverts who prefer to lead by example. But one quality that all great leaders share is humility." They also note the many misconceptions of humility—that it signifies weakness or your people will lose confidence in your leadership abilities, but the opposite is true. They add that humility "allows leaders to listen to others, learn from their mistakes, and develop empathy for their team members. As a result, humility fosters an environment of trust and respect, two essential ingredients for any successful team.[85]

HUMILITY IN LEADERSHIP IS ABOUT PUTTING THE NEEDS OF THE TEAM AND THE ORGANIZATION ABOVE PERSONAL EGO.

Humility is an important trait that involves recognizing and appreciating the contributions of others, being open to feedback, and acknowledging personal limitations. It is not about being weak or lacking confidence but rather having the self-awareness and willingness to learn and grow. Overall, humility in leadership is about putting the needs of the team and the organization above personal ego. It fosters trust, collaboration, and a sense of purpose among team members, ultimately leading to better outcomes and success. Humility should not only be shown to your team but also to the person leading you or the person you report to.

I have seen many leaders lack humility. It exposes their intentions. Those who are not humble, most of the time focus only on themselves. They are prideful and not truly there for the team. They are pretty much there to collect a paycheck. There was a

---

[85] "Humility in Leadership," *Management Consulted*, 17 Nov. 2023, https://managementconsulted.com/humility-in-leadership/#:~:text=Humility%20is%20actually%20a%20strength,ingredients%20for%20any%20successful%20team.

leader whom I encountered early on in aviation, and he pretty much always stayed in his office. He didn't come out much to interact with the team, though he was very friendly. When our executives came around, his behavior would change; suddenly, he was more involved with the team. He would publicly talk to the executives about the great things he had done. He would talk a lot about himself and what he was doing. His behavior made front-line employees feel undervalued because he took all the credit and didn't talk about the team. In another example, one leader I knew was very well-experienced and had been in his role for a long time, but he was a terrible leader. He tried to do everything on his own and put too much on his plate just so that he could say he did it all and take the credit for it. He never delegated. Instead, he played the blame game, accusing his team of laziness and not being proactive. Every conversation was "I, I, I." He was never present with the team and just did his own thing and stroked his ego. He was prideful and didn't empower his team, which is why he was always frustrated that his team wasn't performing well. The problem was a lack of humility.

On the other hand, I have witnessed other leaders nail leading with humility. Eric, my mentor for a long time and a corporate executive for several years, started with the company at age eighteen. Whenever Eric visited, he always interacted more with the front-line team rather than the managers. He asked questions of everyone and was fully invested in their lives outside of work. It can be highly intimidating to encounter a corporate executive, but he made the team feel comfortable because of his ability to connect with them. He would even step in to help with the operation if he saw that the team was too busy and stretched too thin.

He was very open and transparent about current events within the company, and he always asked for feedback. I loved that about him, and I was able to give him honest feedback because he gave me that permission.

Pasquale, another dear mentor of mine whom I've mentioned throughout the book, was another very humble leader. He cared about the team. He always solicited feedback. Though he dressed to the nines, he was never afraid to get his hands dirty. He treated the janitor the same as he treated the leaders on his team. He never thought he was above the team, even though he was a superstar leader within the company. He empowered his team to be part of the change he wanted to see.

Humility was in Eric and Pasquale's DNA because they never forgot where they came from. They never forgot where they started, and they never forgot those who helped them along the way. In *Leadership Unleashed,* Todd Bishop advises his readers to never forget where you started as it keeps you humble and hungry.[86] I observed Eric and Pasquale thank those they worked with in the past whenever they encountered them.

I learned the same from my parents. I have never forgotten the professors who helped me enter into the aviation industry. I never forgot my co-workers who advocated for me, trained me, and allowed me to learn more about the business to help me grow.

Frank, another long-time employee at our company, helped train me when I started my first job. He was a long-time employee working for over fifty years with the company. He helped me with everything and advocated for me. Whenever I go back to California, we'll go play a round of golf together. I am so thankful

---

86 Bishop, *Leadership Unleashed.*

for his support to this day, and he continues to follow my journey through social media and cheer me on from a distance.

Another colleague of mine, Tavonte, also cheered me on along the way. We had few staff on the weekends, so he would take the time to train me in operations and guide me to help grow my knowledge. He is still my biggest fan today, and we sometimes meet up for lunch when I'm in California. And let's not forget about Niall, Steve, and so many more. I try my best to be intentional and stay in touch with them because I appreciate the time they took out in their daily lives to pour into my development and growth. As you grow in your leadership, never forget those who have helped you along the way and never forget your humble beginnings.

I wasn't always humble. Most of my mistakes were with those whom I reported to. I remember in my first leadership role, I was a know-it-all and covered up my mistakes because I was so young and felt I had something prove. I put too much on my plate, thinking it would build credibility and trust with my boss, but that backfired. I ended up making some fairly large mistakes and boy did I learn from them. Not only did I have to be open and transparent with my team but also with my leaders. The more open I became, the more questions I asked, and the more honest I got about not knowing certain things, the more my boss put his faith and trust in me.

I had to learn very quickly how to be humble with my team in my first leadership role because they most were not confident that I was the right leader for them. I had to be in it with the team. It was not all about me. It was all about them and that attitude allowed me to be a light for the team. As Tyler Reagin mentions in *The Life-Giving Leader*, "Humility changes the game for leaders and makes you a light."[87] For me, humility started when I practiced it as a front-line employee. I was freshly graduated from college when I started in the aviation industry. As a front-line employee, I had to be in it with the team. I wasn't afraid to get my hands dirty. I worked long hours and was there for the team when they needed me, and I focused on adding value. In my first book, I discussed the journey of owning the room.[88] I got to know everyone on my team on an individual basis. I voiced how I wanted to grow quickly. Even though I was the "golden child" on the team, I learned so much of what I know about the operation and business from other people. My supervisor, David, who had worked for the company for a long time, was willing to provide me with opportunities to learn. He selected me for special operations and tasks, and I gained his trust. I saw so many fresh college graduates get hired and come in with great pride. They were unwilling to be in it with the team. They put themselves above everyone, and poor work ethic and unwillingness to get their hands dirty led them to poor performance and ultimately termination.

Remember, you don't need to be the leader with all the answers. Your first promotion into leadership can get to your head. John Todorovic writes in his article that "a leader can't let their success go to their head, and they must stay grounded no matter what happens. This is one of the most important parts of humility."[89] And this is so true. There are times when I let promotions and success get to my head, yet leadership is bigger than ourselves. As

---

[87] Reagin, *The Life-Giving Leader*, 99.
[88] Singh, *Navigation and Discovery*.
[89] John Todorovic, "Humility in Leadership—8 Reasons Why Being Humble Is So Important" post, LinkedIn, 8 Dec. 2021, https://www.linkedin.com/pulse/humility-leadership-8-reasons-why-being-humble-so-john-s-todorovic.

Tyler Reagin says, humility involves choosing to live for something bigger than yourself. It is all about the people that you are leading.[90] You must have the posture that you don't know all the answers and lean on your team to find them. This could mean a simple "I don't know." Ultimately, the people on your team want to know whether they can trust you. Your team will help you if you are honest about what you don't know. I recall several times of chaos, and I was transparent that I had no idea how we would get through it. The team was more willing to help and contribute than if I had pretended like I knew everything. They knew I was in it and if I was in it, they were willing to be in it as well.

> **THEY KNEW I WAS IN IT AND IF I WAS IN IT, THEY WERE WILLING TO BE IN IT AS WELL.**

The same thing goes for making mistakes. The reality is you will make many mistakes as a leader . . . more than you know. Those mistakes will be both public and private. The question is: how you are going to face these mistakes? In *Leveling Up*, Ryan Leak mentions that there is fear that if we own our mistakes and shortcomings, people will think less of us.[91] Teams may think their leader is not worth following. This is so not true. When you make mistakes and tell your people that you fell short, it will add

---
90 Reagin, *The Life-Giving Leader*.
91 Leak, *Leveling Up*.

to your credibility, not take away from it. Accept responsibility for your mistakes. A humble leader understands that the team they lead is more important than themselves. And don't play the blame game. Take ownership and learn from your mistakes.

HUMILITY IS A STRENGTH, AND IT ALLOWS YOU TO SEE THE VALUE OF OTHERS.

I am reminded of Romans 12:3, "For by the grace given me I say to every one of you: Do not think of yourself more highly than you ought, but rather think of yourself with sober judgment, in accordance with the faith God has distributed to each of you." Faith has kept me grounded and humble through it all. Humility is a strength, and it allows you to see the value of others. It allows people to grow and develop into their full potential. Give credit to others, and you will develop a great workplace culture. Tyler Reagin mentions "humility is the only step in the process of becoming a life-giving leader in which you choose to focus on something outside yourself and your personality. It is the additional influence on your leadership legacy that just might make the largest impact."[92]

So, wherever you are in your journey—whether as a student, front-line employee, new leader, or experienced leader—are you practicing humility? What shifts do you need to make to have

---
[92] Reagin, *The Life-Giving Leader*, 94.

more humility? Start today where you are. Don't start when you become a leader. Take small steps now. Humility is so countercultural that people take notice when they see it. Humble leaders are rare, and they give people a perfect connection to the bigger story.

CHAPTER 11
LEARN FROM LEADERS

Learning from other leaders is essential for you as you find your way into leadership and continue to grow. I have learned so much from leaders throughout my experience in the aviation industry and other leaders whom I have encountered. You can learn from both good and bad leaders. Learning from other leaders never ends. Once you find your leadership style, your leadership will develop over time. Be observant of how other leaders interact with the team. I tend to be very observant of leaders everywhere I go, whether at the grocery store, out to eat, the bank, or any other establishments—anywhere where you can see leaders interacting with their team or customers.

While some leaders are beacons of support for their teams, I have encountered many other leaders who were very transactional. They were primarily concerned with what they could get out of me and the rest of the team. They didn't care about my well-being. It was all about output and micromanagement. Some of these leaders never followed through with their word. It was difficult to trust them because they didn't manage the business properly. Some leaders didn't treat the customers well and instead manipulated them into doing business with us or charged them extra just because they could. Not surprisingly, many of these leaders did not appreciate their team nor recognize their value.

I am going to take you through the leaders I look up to (many of whom are my close mentors), those who demonstrated poor leadership, and what I learned from them.

THE GOOD LEADER
Steve

Steve hired me into my first leadership role. He also wrote the foreword for this book. He invested time into my development and helped me learn the business and navigate the chaos we were facing at the time. Steve was highly involved with the team and at all levels of the organization. In fact, he spent most of his time out in the operation and developing and empowering his supervisors to make decisions on their own. I also saw him create positions based on the needs of the organization and develop people into those new roles. He was focused on developing people. He was not afraid to hold people accountable and have those difficult conversations. He was not afraid to make tough decisions even if it meant the team would be upset with him. He also did a great job at appreciating and recognizing the team. I learned how he navigated customer relationships during tough times. He was all about continuing to develop relationships with the customers even when things weren't going well. I learned his communication styles through listening to how he spoke on the phone, how he wrote emails, and how he communicated with the team. I remember watching his every move because I wanted to learn everything from him that I could.

Eric

Eric has been my long-time mentor and an executive for the company that I started within the aviation industry. As I mentioned in a previous chapter, Eric started with the company as a front-line employee when he was eighteen and worked his way up to the executive role. Eric never forgot where he came from. He was so humble. He dressed very well but also took great interest in talking to the front-line team members. He always asked questions to get feedback and bounced off ideas about what he was working on at the corporate level. Because of his curiosity and how open he was, the team was comfortable being honest with him, including myself. Anytime he visited, he was very intentional about spending time with the team and didn't put himself above others. He also gave opportunities for further development and training to the top performers and to those who wanted to grow. He would send people to special events so that they could continue to learn and develop themselves.

Eric provided me with countless opportunities to attend conferences and special events, and he helped me succeed in startup locations and integrate newly acquired locations. Even after I left the organization, Eric still made time for me. We have come to be great friends and are now mentors to each other. One thing I have learned from Eric is his intentionality—he's not just going through the motions as an executive. He is very intentional in everything he does whether it be spending time with the team, providing development opportunities, and giving his time to mentor me. You can learn more about Eric in episode 1 of my podcast, *Navigation and Discovery with Cameron Singh*.

Pasquale

I came under Pasquale's mentorship and leadership when I relocated to New Jersey. He taught me so much about senior leadership. Pasquale had strong people skills, and it showed in the way he led the team. He was also very strong on the business side of his role. I saw how he led leadership meetings and other team meetings. I saw how he dealt with customers on the phone, through email, and in person, and I saw how he handled difficult conversations with them. I observed how he communicated with the executive he reported to. I observed how he went above and beyond for corporate visitors and made sure they were treated well and looked after. I learned how to build a budget and manage a profit and loss statement. I learned how to maximize revenues, attract sales, and negotiate. I learned so many business and personal skills from Pasquale, such as finding balance. Pasquale is a huge family man, and it was valuable to learn how he found a healthy work-life balance.

Niall

I worked with Niall in Southern California. He was an awesome Aussie and oversaw a large operation with his teams in several locations at the airport. To have a strong operation, we needed efficient processes in place and a strong leadership team. I learned a lot from Niall on how to develop other leaders and put processes in place to help streamline communications and collect data. Niall provided me with great autonomy and supported me through the implementation of my ideas to develop our leadership team and streamline processes. I also saw how close he was to the customers and how he navigated through difficult situations. He gave me the autonomy to handle many of the difficult situations, whether it was with customers or with our team members. I learned how to go on my own. We had a very new leadership team at the time, and Niall gave me the freedom to do what I needed to help develop and train the new leaders.

Kenny

My first manager was Kenny. He hired me onto my first job in the industry and I worked closely with him through my time in front-line and new leadership roles. Kenny came from a military background as an officer in the Navy. A lot of his leadership style came from his experience in the military. Kenny would start bright and early, and his first stop was not his office. His first stop was to check in with the team, see how the operation was going, and inquire how the day was looking. He made it a priority to spend time with the team. As I mentioned in an earlier chapter, Kenny was in it with the team when we had staff or operations constraints. He wasn't afraid to roll up his sleeves and help out. He always remained calm no matter how crazy things got at work.

Another trait that I look up to is how he never took work home. It was obvious because he never brought anything from home to work, and he never left work with anything. His hands were always free. One day, I asked him why he didn't carry a briefcase or anything. He said, "Work will always be there tomorrow." I took that to heart because I recall seeing so many leaders, including myself, take work home and work until the late hours when they couldn't get everything done at the office. I also learned from him to hire the right people and to give them the resources they need and the autonomy to execute. He taught me that team members who don't execute properly must be held accountable.

Michael

Michael was a top executive with our company, and I landed my first leadership role at our sister company through him. Michael became a close mentor of mine. His mentorship was such a privilege because he was many steps ahead and had a different leadership mindset. I learned to pick apart the mindset of an experienced executive. He was so innovative in the way he explained his past decisions. He stuck to his guns about how to take the company to the next level even when there was pushback. He faced a lot of criticism during his tenure as an executive. I learned to do new and different things that no one has ever done. I learned to go against the grain and norms regardless of what people think of me. Michael is also involved in several new ventures beyond aviation, which inspired me to diversify my interests, as well. My interest in branching out is the reason I wrote this book, launched a real estate company a few years ago, and am now a partner in a new leadership training and coaching company.

Take some time to reflect on the good traits of the leaders you look up to. What traits do you want to incorporate into your leadership? Can you think of anyone who carries the same traits as described in these various leaders?

THE POOR LEADER

You don't want to follow leaders who make everything all about them and not about the team. I will use pseudonyms for these leaders.

Alpha

Alpha spent far too much time in his office. He was on the computer all the time and never helped in times of need. He had minimal interaction with the team. However, when corporate executives came to visit, he was so different. He would be more involved with the team and take credit for things that the team was doing. It was all about him and making himself look good.

Bravo

Bravo didn't last long. He was very selfish, knew nothing about the business, and never really took the time to learn. He mastered his work in the office and made a big ethical mistake that led to his termination within a few short months of starting his new role.

Charlie

Charlie was experienced and had worked his way up in the company, yet he never delegated properly. Instead, he would fill up his plate and do everything on his own without asking the team to help. Then he would get upset with the team and accuse them of laziness. He took all the credit for the team's accomplishments. He ended the day exhausted. His team members and leadership team often couldn't find him when they needed him because he didn't communicate well.

LESSONS LEARNED

Aim to learn from both good and bad leaders—take on the good traits from the good and avoid what the bad leaders do. You will find many strategies are adaptable to your leadership style, while others may be ineffective for the way you lead. Either way, maintain the posture of learning from other leaders.

ELEVATE YOUR LEADERSHIP. LEARN FROM THE GOOD AND THE BAD.

I ask leaders question after question to try and get into their minds on how they lead, why they lead, the mistakes they made, and why they are so successful in leadership. John F. Kennedy once said, "Leadership and learning are indispensable to each other."[93] Elevate your leadership. Learn from the good and the bad.

---

93 John F. Kennedy, "Leadership and learning are indispensable to each other," *Remarks at Trade Mart in Dallas, TX,* 22 Nov. 1963, https://www.jfklibrary.org/archives/other-resources/john-f-kennedy-speeches/dallas-tx-trade-mart-undelivered-19631122.

CHAPTER 12
DON'T LOSE YOURSELF IN LEADERSHIP

Leadership is not easy. It comes with a great weight and burden. As Dr. Sam Chand says in his book *Turbo Leadership*, "Leadership is not a role. It is not something you do. It's a responsibility related to who you are."[94] You can easily lose yourself in leadership if you chase validation and place your identity in advances within your career. After my first promotion, I embarked on a trajectory of growth and was able to grow quickly in various roles. I moved from state to state and abroad within a short period of time, but I lost myself and forgot who I was because I was consistently in the spotlight. I was yearning for the next spotlight and for the next accolade. There were times when I just went through the motions of leadership, especially during difficult times when I woke up at 5 a.m. to be at work early and then stayed until the late hours of the night. Sometimes, I even nodded off on the drive home! Things became too much for me to handle and I didn't want to seek the help I needed from my boss because it would make me

---
94 Chand, *Turbo Leadership*.

feel inferior. I also feared that seeking help would confirm to my boss that I was too young or underdeveloped to lead well.

I felt a great deal of pressure in these prestigious leadership roles. Many other leaders in similar roles worked longer and waited for years until they finally landed these leadership roles. Many doubted me and the pressures just took over. The pressures of leadership slowly began to consume me. It was unhealthy and negatively impacted both my professional and personal life.

As I've mentioned throughout the book, I find it important to remember why you chose to pursue leadership in the first place. Why do you want it? Why did you choose the industry or field that you did? Why did you choose the school that you did? Why are you working in the job you are in today?

BE CAREFUL NOT TO CHANGE TO CONFORM TO THE NORMS.

People took a risk on me, believed in me, and saw something I did not see in myself. I want to do the same for others. I want people to see they have greater potential than they think. Don't lose sight of your why. I made my why visible at my work and home office. I would re-read my personal mission statement as a reminder to center myself and return to why I am doing what I am doing. It would remind me of my purpose and what I needed to do to get to where I am today.

Be careful not to change to conform to the norms. Go against the norms. Be innovative. Look for other ways of doing things to elevate your team and business. Be bold. Get out of your comfort zone. Set yourself apart. Do what you need to do and trust your gut.

I am proud that I have always stayed true to myself. I never tried to change. I never conformed to the crowd. Anna Bebutova wrote a post on her LinkedIn page that said, "knowing the real you is as important as understanding your values. It means being honest when identifying what you love about yourself, and what you want to work on."[95]

THE SPOTLIGHT CAN DO ONE OF TWO THINGS: SWALLOW YOU UP OR BUILD YOUR TEAM UP.

You will probably face a lot of criticism and negativity. People will insist that you do the basics and discourage innovation. In one chapter of *Leadership Unleashed*, Todd Bishop writes about "screwing" what other people think: "If you are called to lead, you are going to have to screw what other people think. The moment you step out in front of the pack is when criticism and cynicism are launched at you."[96] So many people advised me to just do my job and fly under the radar. But that wasn't me; I wanted to do things

---
95 Anna Bebutova, "Never Lose Sight of Yourself post, *LinkedIn*, 19 Feb. 2019, https://www.linkedin.com/pulse/never-lose-sight-yourself-anna-bebutova-cam-.
96 Bishop, *Leadership Unleashed*.

that we had never done because that is what would add value to my team and the company at large. I'm not a "stay under the radar" kind of guy. God has put me on this earth to shine a light. I tend to be in the spotlight often, but it hasn't always served me. The spotlight can do one of two things: swallow you up or build your team up. My faith has kept me grounded. Matthew 10:30 states "Whoever finds their own life will lose it, and whoever loses their life for my sake will find it." When you live from a place of faith, you live for something much bigger than your life and your business.

My purpose is to love people and share the love that God shares with us. I live out my faith through the work that I do. Faith may not be a part of your life or you may be closed off to faith or exploring faith. My faith allows me to believe in a higher purpose. There's a higher purpose in leading people. There's a higher purpose in leadership. In the *Maxwell Leadership Bible*, John Maxwell instructs leaders *not* to allow the discontent of the masses to influence your assignment and to instead take direction from God only and stay committed to the mission He has set for you because leaders build trust by sharing in the struggles of their people.[97] "Don't let your mandate come from the grumbling of the crowd. Get your cues from God and the mission He has given you. Leaders gain credibility when they suffer with those they lead." Galatians 1:10 (NLT) says "Obviously I'm not trying to win the approval of people, but of God. If pleasing people were my goal, I would not be Christ's servant."

Are you trying to win the approval of people? What are you going after? Does their approval really matter? Is there something more important than the approval of people?

---
[97] John C. Maxwell, *Maxwell Leadership Bible* (Nashville, TN: Thomas Nelson, March 12, 2019).

In a previous chapter, I mentioned Kenny who never took anything home and never brought anything to work. His hands were always empty. I learned a great lesson from him when he said, "Work will always be there tomorrow." I have found myself many times working long hours to complete in one day all the work I need done, but the reality is that your work will be there tomorrow. Work isn't everything.

YOU MAY FIND YOURSELF SPENDING TOO MUCH TIME AND ENERGY ON WORK THAT DOESN'T MATTER AND ADDS VERY LITTLE VALUE TO THE BIG PICTURE.

Yes, leadership is important and we need to be there for the people we lead. We need stable income and could always use more. Yet there is more to life. Remember the rock exercise I mentioned in Chapter 1? Through this exercise, I realized that my leadership and influence extended far beyond work and into other spaces such as my community, family, friends, and much more. We have to find a balance that works for us, but I know—it is easier said than done. I like the way Christy Wright thinks about balance. In Episode 4 of my podcast, she mentioned that balance is all about finding your balance and redefining it to what fits best for you.[98] This means that there will be busy periods and busy sea-

---
98 Wright, "Take Back Your Time."

sons where you will need to work long hours. It's all about working towards what matters most. You may find yourself spending too much time and energy on work that doesn't matter and adds very little value to the big picture. We need to be very intentional about the work we do so we can find that work-life balance and have the most impact possible in every sphere of our lives.

CHAPTER 13

CONTINUAL DEVELOPMENT AND EDUCATION

Chapter 1 of my first book discusses how continuing education was a part of my leadership journey.[99] I am a huge champion of higher education, and for me, education will never end, and it should never end for you, either, especially if you are new to leadership. My hunger for continual development and education has never diminished. If you do not grow as a leader, your leadership will become stagnant. You have to continuously fill your tank with education to lead and pour into the people you lead. What are you doing today to develop and educate yourself? What type of content are you consuming?

You may scroll through TikTok and Instagram for countless hours. And there's time for that. I sometimes get sucked into it, too—scrolling for hours upon hours—but constant consumption of social media can become very dangerous and inhibit your opportunities for development and education.

---
99 Singh, *Navigation and Discovery.*

The content that you consume matters. I choose to follow all the podcasters, pastors, leaders, and motivational speakers that I look up to on social media so that the majority of the content I see on social media is helping me grow. Not only do I consume it, but I also share it to encourage people wherever they are. That's another to keep in mind: *share* what you are learning whether on public platforms or in-person with your team. While consuming social media doesn't have to sink you, beware of the content you consume and be intentional about who you choose to follow.

Of course, the primary source of education is through formal means, like a four-year university or community college. I have always enjoyed school, so pursuing education through the highest level of graduate school worked in my favor. Even if higher education isn't your thing, you must find ways to grow and mature in your area of leadership expertise.

You can also take online courses or attend conferences and other events. Continuing education doesn't always have to focus on your line of work or leadership. In fact, growing within the industry actually depends on development in other areas, which is why I continuously seek to develop myself in domains of life. Conferences are a great way to hear different perspectives on how to elevate my leadership. I went through the Maxwell Leadership Certification program to become a certified leadership speaker, trainer, and coach. To this day, I still attend the leadership and faith-based conferences that I have mentioned throughout this book. These trainings have led into other business pursuits. I have learned about real estate through online courses and in-person workshops and started a real estate investment business a few years ago. These courses walked me through the process of developing the business and taught me all its intricacies. Reading has also helped me further my education. I love reading books and learning more about faith and leadership. I never leave a bookstore without purchasing a book. I always find something in an area I want to learn more about.

YOU NEVER KNOW WHAT OPPORTUNITIES CAN COME YOUR WAY WITH CONTINUOUS CURIOSITY.

Online research and magazines are also good forms of education. Many of the interviews on my podcast and the podcasts that I co-host have surprised me—some of the leaders do not read. They consume their content through online research and magazines. The AVAIL journal is one of my favorite magazines, as it intersects faith and leadership. It is a quarterly journal with rich and refreshing leadership content.

You can refer to the Appendix at the end of this book for a list of podcasts, books, and magazines that I regularly read or subscribe to. Keep current in your industry. Seek further education on everything that interests you, not just your work. You never know what opportunities can come your way with continuous curiosity. For example, my interest in real estate started when I purchased a new home and then had to move six months later. I didn't want to sell the home, so I decided to list it as a short-term rental. All it took was a little research to spark the idea of building an entire real estate investment business and generating passive income in other ways. Keep learning and educating yourself, and stay curious!

FINAL THOUGHTS
DON'T GIVE UP. PRESS ON. KEEP LEADING.

Carey Nieuwhof mentions that "the weight of leadership never leaves leaders. The wise ones learn how to deal with it."[100] How true is that statement?! The weight of leadership is so great and over time, it can take a real toll on a new leader. My first years of leadership were such a whirlwind. I went through so much to figure out my leadership style, how to lead myself, and how to lead people. Leading people is not easy, and leading yourself is even more difficult. The pressures are many as a leader: the pressure to perform, the pressure to take care of your team, the pressure to hold them accountable, and the pressure of making money and budgeting appropriately. It's overwhelming.

The reality is that you are going to make mistakes. You are going to fail more times than you can count. Learn from those mistakes and failures and continue to press on. You will become a better leader for every mistake and failure you face. Times will

---
100 Carey Nieuwhof, "9 Hidden Things That Make or Break Leaders," *Carey Nieuwhof Blog*, https://careynieuwhof.com/9-hidden-things-that-make-or-break-leaders/.

get tough, especially when you face failure. You'll feel discouraged. You'll question why you chose the path you did. You'll question whether it is all worth it. You'll question whether you made the right choice when you applied for that promotion. You'll question whether you chose the right line of work. You have to continue to press on, learn from the mistakes and failures, and move forward. You will feel like giving up. You will feel like quitting. I thought of quitting my job several times in the different leadership roles I've held. You will feel like you don't belong in your role.

GO AFTER FAILURE RATHER THAN BEING AFRAID OF IT.

Press on! Be the best leader that you can be each and every day! You have people to lead. Make sure you take care of yourself first and find whatever balance works for you. This may take some time. You'll face criticism. You'll face negativity. People around you won't feel that you deserve your position. People will wait for you to fail.

Go after failure rather than being afraid of it. As John Maxwell frequently says—fail forward. Learn from the failure and move onto the next failure. That is how you grow and develop as a leader.

Stay focused on your why. It's very easy to get lost in all the noise that comes with leadership. Remember why you wanted to step into leadership in the first place.

The people you surround yourself with matter a lot. Surround yourself with people who help you elevate. Seek mentors who will support you and hold you accountable. I tend to keep my inner circle small, and I look for relationships where value is added both ways. Through my journey, many people have just wanted something from me rather than a genuine relationship.

THE RIGHT PEOPLE WILL HELP YOU FAIL FORWARD AND LEARN THINGS THAT YOU HAD NEVER CONSIDERED BEFORE.

The right people will help you fail forward and learn things that you had never considered before. They will give you the grace you need to push past the pain and strive for higher. They will carry you on their shoulders when everyone else walks out.

The weight of leadership in today's world is heavier than ever. Leadership is not an easy journey; but it's a blessing because you are divinely positioned to change lives. You can change the trajectory of a business. You can develop people. You can help people see the potential in themselves that no one else has ever seen in them. You can help put someone through school. Your influence as a leader can have a huge impact. The highs of being a leader are just that—changing lives and helping people grow. If you can just change one person's life through your leadership, it is all worth it!

So don't give up, press on, and keep leading!

IF YOU CAN JUST CHANGE ONE PERSON'S LIFE THROUGH YOUR LEADERSHIP, IT IS ALL WORTH IT!

APPENDIX

I am happy to connect with you if you need any support, have any questions, or just want to have a chat. I am also available for keynotes and speaking engagements along with leadership development for teams and organizations. You can send me an email at singhcameron@outlook.com.

You will find a wide range of resources on my website, www.CameronSingh.com that is constantly evolving, including podcasts, the DiSC assessment, lists of books, magazines, and more. Here are the podcasts that I host and co-host presently:

- The Leadership Download Podcast
- The Executive Leadership Podcast
- Navigation and Discovery with Cameron Singh
- Divine Revelations Unleashed (see website for more information)

If you have not yet read my first book *Navigation and Discovery*, I would encourage you to get a copy of it to learn more about my story.

If this book was an encouragement for you and know someone else who needs to hear this message, gift them a copy of this book and encourage them that, yes, they can be a leader!

ABOUT THE AUTHOR

Cameron Nathan Singh's journey is a testament to the power of determination and passion. Born and raised in San Bruno, California, Cameron's early years laid the foundation for his future endeavors.

With a keen enthusiasm for leadership and a drive to make a meaningful impact on younger generations, Cameron found his calling in the business aviation industry growing up by San Francisco International Airport. His career trajectory has been nothing short of remarkable, marked by a rapid ascent up the corporate ladder over the past decade. He has had the opportunity to live in places such as New Jersey, Southern California, and Chicago to the tranquil shores of the Caribbean twin islands of Antigua and Barbuda. Cameron's professional journey has taken him across diverse landscapes, both literal and figurative.

Equipped with a Doctorate of Executive Leadership from the University of Charleston, Cameron embodies a rare blend of academic prowess and real-world experience.

Beyond his corporate achievements, Cameron is a multifaceted individual with a passion for communication and mentorship. As the host and co-host of several podcasts, he leverages the power of storytelling to share insights and lessons learned from his own leadership journey. A certified coach, speaker, and trainer under the guidance of John C. Maxwell, Cameron is dedicated to nurturing the next generation of leaders.

Cameron is also the Director of Curriculum and Assistant Professor for the Aviation Science program at California Baptist University in Southern California where he currently resides.

In addition to his podcasting endeavors, Cameron is also an accomplished author, with his book *Navigation and Discovery: A Path of Navigating and Discovering Through Your Journey of Faith* serving as a beacon of guidance for those seeking direction in their personal and professional lives.

At the core of Cameron's endeavors lies a profound desire to instill a sense of purpose and ambition in young minds. His unwavering commitment to mentorship and leadership development underscores his belief in the transformative power of guidance and inspiration. Through his own journey, Cameron seeks to ignite a spark of ambition in others and encourage them to chart their own course towards success and fulfillment.

Cameron is available for speaking engagements, training workshops, and coaching.

You can find out more at www.CameronSingh.com where you can find his social media profiles.

Email: singhcameron@outlook.com